COMMON
VALUES

COMMON
CAUSE

COMMON
VALUES

COMMON
CAUSE

**German Statesmen in the United States
American Statesmen in Germany
1953—1983
Statements and Speeches**

Published 1983 by the
German Information Center
410 Park Avenue
New York, N.Y. 10022

ISBN: 0-912685-03-4 (hard cover)
0-912685-04-2 (paperback)

Library of Congress Catalog Card Number: 83-83024

Produced by Fred Weidner & Son Printers, Inc.
Design by Creative Images in Inc.

Foreword

Thirty years ago, in April 1953, Chancellor Konrad Adenauer became the first German head of government to visit the United States. Adenauer's visit, four years after the founding of the Federal Republic of Germany, began a long series of meetings between German and American statesmen on both sides of the Atlantic which have highlighted a relationship of close cooperation between the two countries going beyond simple calculations of national interest. That cooperation originated in the generous assistance given by the United States to the German people after the end of the Second World War, and in America's support for the new republic. It is based on the awareness that common efforts are necessary to guarantee common security. It is based on common values and a common cause.

The speeches and statements in this book underscore the great importance which the United States and Germany attach to the bonds between them and reflect the endeavours of eight American presidents and six German chancellors to strengthen them. Whatever the changes in leadership and government, those bonds have been forged into a permanent element of the political life of both nations. This documentation attests to the continuity of their relationship, the quality of their cooperation, and the identity of their interests, transcending all legitimate, and passing, differences of opinion.

This partnership needs to be nurtured on a broad basis. The German government and the American administration therefore welcome all efforts which serve to expand mutual contacts and to pass on to younger generations that sense of interdependence and partnership which inspired a generation still influenced by the experience of the war.

This year 1983 marks the tricentennial of the first German immigration to America. More than fifty million Americans claim German descent, and German-Americans have provided major contributions to every aspect of American life. The joint celebration of the tricentennial is, to quote President Reagan, "a visible sign of United States and German friendship and the strength of our partnership." The visit of Federal President Carstens to the United States in October 1983 continued a political tradition which began 30 years ago with the visit of Konrad Adenauer.

Washington, D.C.
December 1983

Peter Hermes
Ambassador of the
Federal Republic of Germany

Table of Contents

page

1 Statement by Chancellor Adenauer April 7, 1953, on His Arrival in Washington 1

2 Speech by Chancellor Adenauer at the Commonwealth Club in San Francisco, April 11, 1953 3

3 Statement by Chancellor Adenauer Upon Signing the Treaty on Friendship, Commerce, and Navigation, October 29, 1954 8

4 Joint Statement of June 14, 1955, on the Occasion of the Meeting Between President Dwight D. Eisenhower and Chancellor Adenauer 10

5 Address by Chancellor Adenauer at Yale University, June 11, 1956 11

6 Chancellor Adenauer's Senate Address, May 27, 1957 17

7 Chancellor Adenauer's Address to the U.S. House of Representatives, May 28, 1957 21

8 Joint Declaration of May 28, 1957, Concerning the Discussions Between President Eisenhower and Chancellor Adenauer 25

9 Welcoming Remarks by President Eisenhower to President Heuss, June 5, 1958 28

10 Address by President Heuss Before the U.S. Congress, June 6, 1958 30

11 Joint Statement on the Occasion of President Eisenhower's Visit of August 27, 1958 36

12 Joint Communiqué After the Meeting Between President Kennedy and Chancellor Adenauer, November 22, 1961 37

13 Remarks by Chancellor Adenauer and President Kennedy at Welcoming Ceremonies in Bonn, June 23, 1963 40

14 Toasts by President Kennedy and Chancellor Adenauer at a Dinner on June 24, 1963 43

15 Joint Communiqué of June 24, 1963 46

16 Speech by President Kennedy in the Paulskirche in Frankfurt, June 25, 1963 48

17 President Kennedy in Berlin, June 26, 1963 57

18 Address by Chancellor Erhard in New York,
June 11, 1964 60

19 Dinner Speech by Chancellor Erhard on the Occasion of
His Meeting With President Johnson,
September 26, 1966 71

20 Joint Statement Following Discussions Between
President Johnson and Chancellor Erhard,
September 27, 1966 74

21 Remarks by President Johnson and
Chancellor Kiesinger at Welcoming Ceremonies
in Washington, August 15, 1967 80

22 President Nixon's Address to the German Parliament,
February 26, 1969 85

23 Welcoming Ceremony for Chancellor Brandt,
April 10, 1970 88

24 Remarks by Chancellor Brandt April 10, 1970, at a
Dinner Given by President Nixon 91

25 Address by Chancellor Brandt at Harvard University on
June 5, 1972, Twenty-Five Years After the
Announcement of the Marshall Plan 95

26 Exchange of Remarks Between President Ford and
Chancellor Schmidt, December 5, 1974 107

27 Visit of President Scheel to the United States,
June 16, 1975 110

28 President Scheel's Address Before Congress,
June 17, 1975 114

29 Exchange of Toasts Between President Ford and
President Scheel, July 27, 1975 120

30 Speech by Chancellor Schmidt at Johns Hopkins
University, July 16, 1976 124

31 Remarks by Chancellor Schmidt July 13, 1977, on the
Occasion of his Meeting With President Carter 132

32 Speech by President Carter During His Visit to Bonn,
July 14, 1978 137

33 Statements by President Reagan and Chancellor
Schmidt at Their Meeting on May 21, 1981 142

34 Joint Statement of May 22, 1981, on the Occasion of
Chancellor Schmidt's Visit 146

35 Address by President Reagan Before the Bundestag
in Bonn, June 9, 1982 149

36 Address by President Reagan to the People of Berlin,
June 11, 1982 158

37 Remarks by President Reagan and Chancellor Kohl
on the Chancellor's Arrival in Washington,
November 15, 1982 164

38 Joint Statement by President Reagan and Chancellor
Kohl, November 16, 1982 169

39 Speech by Chancellor Kohl Before the American
Council on Germany in New York,
November 16, 1982 177

40 Statement by Chancellor Kohl in Washington,
April 15, 1983 182

41 Remarks by President Reagan in an Exchange of Toasts
With President Carstens at a White House State Dinner,
October 4, 1983 185

42 Speech by President Carstens in Response to President
Reagan's Remarks, October 4, 1983 187

43 Address by President Carstens to a Joint Session of
Congress, October 5, 1983 190

44 Speech by President Carstens at the Tricentennial
Banquet in Philadelphia, October 6, 1983 196

45 Speech by President Carstens at Carnegie Hall,
New York, October 13, 1983 199

Sources 203

1

Statement by Chancellor Adenauer April 7, 1953, on His Arrival in Washington

Chancellor Adenauer at airport press conference with Vice President Nixon (left) and Secretary of State Dulles (right) in Washington April 7, 1953.

On April 7, 1953, Chancellor Konrad Adenauer arrived in Washington for his first visit to the United States. It was the first visit ever by a German head of goverment.

To the welcoming statements by Vice President Richard Nixon and Secretary of State John Foster Dulles, Dr. Adenauer responded as follows:

Mr. Vice-President, Mr. Secretary:

I am entering your capital with deep emotion. You have addressed such cordial and meaningful words to us and the German people that I find it difficult to answer adequately. You, Mr. Vice-President, have spoken of General Steuben. I want to thank you for having gone back to the early past of long years of cooperation, gallantly disregarding the last decade.

1

You, Mr. Secretary, have joined the Vice-President in speaking of the new tasks ahead, of the work to be done, the sacrifices to be made and the goals to be reached by all men of goodwill who consider liberty, right and justice as the most precious possessions of humanity and who are ready to devote all their efforts to securing them. In this memorable moment, please accept from me this solemn declaration: the German people want liberty, the German people want right and justice for all nations.

I myself, and I know the German people support me in this, am deeply grateful to your honored President for making possible a frank and open exchange of opinions on the questions which concern us in these turbulent times. Above all, however, let me—as the representative of the German people—thank your President and the American people with all my heart for the help they have extended during the postwar years to the German people, in a spirit of genuine human understanding. We shall never forget that. We shall always be your true and faithful partners on the difficult road by which the United States is leading mankind to freedom.

Finally, Mr. Secretary, may I add that I remember with great pleasure our meeting in Bonn and our frank and open talks there. I am looking forward to continuing them here, and I anticipate with the utmost pleasure the opportunity of seeing your President again whose activities as the head of NATO forces in Europe I have always held in great esteem.

2

Speech by Chancellor Adenauer at the Commonwealth Club in San Francisco, April 11, 1953

Dr. Adenauer also visited San Francisco, Chicago, New York, and Cambridge, Massachusetts, on his first trip to the United States. On April 11, 1953, he made the following speech at a luncheon hosted by the Commonwealth Club in San Francisco:

Ladies and Gentlemen:

I am delighted to be with you today, and I want to thank your Chairman for this opportunity to get to know you better and to exchange some views with you.

Two reasons prompted me to come here: one political and one personal. The political consideration was that San Francisco is the great gateway to the Pacific area and to the Far East. You face the Asiatic continent and for this reason California is mainly interested in questions dealing with the Orient.

I am a German and a European, and Europe is therefore my main concern. But all of us must be clear that in this period of worldwide tension the questions of the Far East and of Europe are most closely interwoven and that one cannot be settled without the other. I think, therefore, that my best approach would be to try to sketch for you the situation in Europe.

The Two Fronts

I know that your thoughts are now with the Korean truce negotiations on which in large measure depend further world developments. In fact, you have very special interests in these negotiations: through your city have passed the long lines of soldiers and sailors who went to fight in this undeclared war, and through your port have returned the sad cargoes of the wounded and maimed. I want to tell you that we in Germany know that your boys are fighting for our freedom as well as yours and that of the other free nations. We are grateful for their sacrifices and we join with you in your hopes and prayers that the end of the fighting may soon arrive.

We are holding another front, with your people, with France and Britain. Straight across our land runs an arbitrary line which, since 1945, has represented the line between East and West, between liberty and despotism. Almost half our country and a third of our

3

population live under Communist domination. Our former capital of Berlin is an island in a red sea. Those who have never lived under a totalitarian system cannot have any conception of what it means to be helplessly and hopelessly exposed to a brutal and godless dictatorship, which respects no personal freedom, has unlimited power at its disposal, and which places no value on the individual. The Germans in the Soviet zone suffer the most severe physical and emotional deprivations, but they have given up neither their resistance nor their hope.

Subversion From The East

Out of East Germany flows an incessant and tragic stream of refugees into the Federal Republic. When life becomes completely unbearable for them, they leave behind their belongings, house and property, and come to us. During the past two years, over two million people have fled under these circumstances. If you can imagine what it means to give up your home, your work, your household, your farm, which in many instances has been in the hands of one family for generations, you will understand how desperate these people must be. They know that they face no rosy future when they come to us in the West.

Our country is overpopulated. Within the past few years, over eight million people were pressed into our country, so that one out of five citizens is a refugee. This overpopulation of the Federal Republic, it seems to me, is a Soviet move deliberately designed to shatter our social and economic structure and to make possible Communist subversion, which flourishes during social and economic upheaval. We in the Federal Republic are one of the main targets of the Soviet-inspired cold war. Up to now, we have uncovered approximately 250 Communist-front organizations in our country. Only recently we uncovered and destroyed one of the most dangerous and far-reaching Soviet spy rings, after we had already unearthed a Polish and a Czech spy ring. This unbroken and steadily continuing activity against subversion is one part of defense in the cold war. But that isn't all. The social and economic reconstruction of Germany, the securing of our democratic heritage, are further bulwarks of this defense.

Countermeasures

Communism must be fought with spiritual weapons as well. The tendency toward de-individualization is only too closely tied up with the rise of modern technology. The suppression of personality, the massing of people opens the way towards a totalitarian state.

4

We are doing our best to counter it in all spheres of education. But however essential all these measures are, they alone are insufficient.

The available armed forces in Western Europe are in no wise sufficient to discourage Soviet attack, since 140 divisions are garrisoned in the Soviet zone and western Russia, and 60 to 70 divisions more in the satellite countries, all fully equipped with modern arms. This strong military pressure from the East is the immediate reason for the signing of the European Defense Community Treaty between Italy, France, Belgium, Holland, Luxembourg and the Federal Republic of Germany. The treaty was signed by all participating countries in May, 1952. Unfortunately, with the sole exception of the German Bundestag, the parliaments of the signatory powers have not yet ratified it, although time is of the essence and the satellite states are steadily rearming.

I am of the opinion that Soviet Russia will consider serious discussions aimed towards a sincere relaxation of tensions only when she realizes that the West will not be deterred from its plans of unification and combined strength. I hold the speedy ratification of the European Defense Communty Treaty to be a most essential, even a decisive, prerequisite to fruitful conferences with the Soviet Union. Once the unification of the West has become an accomplished fact, one can assume that Soviet Russia will think twice before using the largest part of its production for armament, thus neglecting the production of consumer goods for its own people.

Even if current tensions disappeared or were greatly diminished, the uniting of the West European nations into a common defense effort and the eventual political union would still be necessary. As a result of the two wars, the distribution of power has been greatly changed. The Soviet bloc is too strong, the West European nations by themselves too weak. Such an imbalance constantly risks overweighting of political and military power. In the long run, the unification of Western Europe along military, political and economic lines is therefore a necessity.

The United States has long recognized this necessity, and considers it the first step towards the establishment of a stable relationship. Therefore, you promote unification.

We are very grateful to you. We Europeans, as a result of our traditions, are heavily burdened with sympathies, antipathies which are no longer current. Frequently we are held too strongly to the traditions of the past. But we do make progress even though there are difficulties arising out of the past which sometimes even block the road to a united Europe. But with your help, we shall succeed.

I have tried to sketch for you the cold war to which we in

5

Germany are particularly exposed, to show you how the free nations of Europe, and particularly we in Germany as the nearest neighbors to communism, do all we can to fulfill our duty in this contest.

In order to give evidence to you and the whole world that we regard the battle in Korea as one ensuring our freedom as well, the Federal Goverment, prior to my departure, decided to make available to President Eisenhower a field hospital, fully equipped with doctors, nurses, medical supplies, and other necessities. Please regard this as a gesture of our solidarity.

German Problems and Policies

To return to some of our problems which have worldwide as well as domestic repercussions, I should like to comment on the fact that in the press of many nations reports have appeared which would indicate that the Nazi movement in Germany is about to celebrate its renascence, or will do so very shortly. These prophecies must be discounted because they are false.

It is no wonder that after a twelve-year Nazi rule some National Socialists still exist. But they are few because the terrible catastrophe of the collapse opened many eyes and, further, a few Nazis don't make a Nazi-dominated Germany. It is moreover interesting that the small circle of Nazis recently uncovered in Germany was financially backed by French and British National Socialists.

We are firmly resolved not to repeat the mistakes of the Weimar Republic which, by its exaggerated liberalism, permitted the enemies of the country to destroy provisions to deal with individuals and groups which do not abide by the rules of democratic principles. We have already applied these laws to prohibit and dissolve such organizations of the extreme right, and we will apply them against radical elements of both the right and the left. There will not be another 1933.

Recently we concluded a treaty with Israel, in which we agreed to deliver to that country goods to the amount of three billion D-marks. This does not affect compensation for individual victims of the Nazi regime. We signed the treaty with Israel to show the whole world that Germany has broken with one of the elementary principles of National Socialism. The German Bundestag has voted for the treaty with a singularly large majority. I regard the ratification of this treaty as the most emphatic proof of the break with the National Socialist past.

The German-American Relationship

One of the numerous constructive developments during the past year has been the very generous exchange program between Germany and the United States, initiated by your government. Within the framework of this program, thousands of my countrymen, currently in high places in public life, or who will be later, have been given the opportunity to visit this country to study your way of life and your form of democracy. There undoubtedly is no one among these visitors who has not gained much by this experience. Two of my sons took part in this exchange program, and I regard myself on this trip as an exchange student, coming to your country with open eyes and ears.

You know, gentlemen, that I have come from Washington after several conferences with President Eisenhower, Secretary of State Dulles, and other members of your Government. You know of the communiqué which covered the essence of these conferences. I don't want to discuss its content here; it will suffice to emphasize the following:

As you can gather from the communiqué, my conversations with President Eisenhower about the world situation resulted in agreement on a not too optimistic estimate. Our talks on German-American relationships were especially satisfying.

Above all, I am satisfied with the general atmosphere in which my talks with both President Eisenhower and Secretary of State Dulles were held. The conversations were conducted in a spirit of friendliness and cooperation. The final statement, that the talks appreciably contributed toward reaching the common goals of both countries and toward strengthening the free world, will meet with the complete approval of the German people.

I mentioned at the opening of my remarks that I also had a personal reason for visiting you. I wanted to get an idea of the diversity and magnitude of your country, and I wanted to come to California, a trip which has for many years been one of my dreams, because of its history, its beauty, its unique natural wonders. Now that I am here I am enchanted with this wonderful country, its scenery and its sunshine. It pains me that duties call me back so soon. However, I will always carry with me a deep impression of your wonderful country.

3

Statement by Chancellor Adenauer Upon Signing the Treaty on Friendship, Commerce, and Navigation, October 29, 1954

Chancellor Adenauer and President Eisenhower conferring at White House, Washington, October 27, 1954.

Chancellor Adenauer again visited the United States from October 26 to November 3, 1954. On October 29, 1954, he signed the Treaty on Friendship, Commerce, and Navigation. In his introductory remarks Dr. Adenauer referred to the outcome of the Paris Conference held October 19–23, 1954, at which the Federal Republic of Germany was invited to join NATO:

Mr. Secretary, it has been a special pleasure to sign on behalf of the Federal Republic of Germany this treaty of friendship, commerce and navigation which our two governments have negotiated in a constructive spirit. With your appreciative comments on the results of the Paris conference you have expressed my own heartfelt sentiments. The main purpose of our political action is not to deploy

8

armed forces but to strengthen the bonds of friendship within the free world and to enhance the prosperity of our peoples. To our regret we are compelled to build up our military capacity in order to protect these values.

I therefore welcome this treaty as another important contribution toward peaceful co-operation between our two countries. It is a comprehensive and modern commercial and legal instrument intended to give the trade, industry and commerce of both countries, and their citizens, a firm basis for the free development of their economic, cultural and human relationships. I hope that the flow of vital energies that has already re-emerged in recent years from the manifold ties and contacts between the United States of America and Germany will receive fresh, strong impulses from this treaty.

A special aim of the negotiations was to place our mutual economic relations on as liberal a basis as possible and to create favorable conditions for trade. I am therefore convinced that the treaty will prove beneficial to the economic life of both nations.

Of deeper significance is the fact that the Federal Republic of Germany has concluded its first treaty of friendship, commerce and navigation with the great American nation. In recent years and months we have time and again recalled, and rightly so, how important to us, as to the other freedom-loving nations, is the protection afforded by our powerful American friend against the threat to which we are constantly exposed. But at the same time let us not forget that this shield is worth only the values it protects. Within the protected and delimited area we want a rich and beautiful life to prosper, with free nations being able to compete peacefully with one another in a free exchange of their talents and the products of their labor for the benefit of their citizens and for the enhancement of their culture. Those are the convictions which generated the imposing development of the American nation. They are the very ideals which form the basis of our own political and economic life. This identify of ethical foundations is the true source of the friendship that unites our peoples, a friendship, therefore, that is far more than a mere community of interests which owes its existence to a momentary, hopefully a transient danger from outside. Consequently, it is a durable element in the life of our nations. To express this is the chief meaning of the treaty we have just concluded.

4

Joint Statement of June 14, 1955, on the Occasion of the Meeting Between President Dwight D. Eisenhower and Chancellor Adenauer

At the conclusion of the discussions in Washington during Dr. Adenauer's visit to the United States June 12–19, 1955, the following joint statement was issued:

The President, the Chancellor, the Secretary of State and their advisors met this morning and discussed the problems of concern to their two nations. They reviewed the political developments which have taken place since the Chancellor's last visit and noted with satisfaction that bonds of friendship between their nations have become very close. They are of the opinion that the recent favorable developments in Europe are the result of the consistent, sound policies followed by the United States, the Federal Republic and their allies.

A large part of their discussion was devoted to the relationship between the nations of the free world and the Soviet Union and particularly the recent developments such as the willingness of the Soviet Union to participate in the four-power conference and the invitation of the Soviet Government to the Chancellor. They agreed that one of the objectives of the forthcoming four-power meeting will be to pave the way for early German reunification. It was confirmed that in their combined opinion the concept of neutrality is in no way applicable to Germany and that only in collective security arrangements can Germany assure its independence.

As a result of their discussions, they are reassured that there is a very broad field of understanding between them. They are convinced that the achievement of the policies upon which Germany and the United States are embarked will continue to require closest cooperation in the future. These policies are based on a common adherence to the furtherance of a just and enduring peace among the nations of the world.

5

Address by Chancellor Adenauer at Yale
University, June 11, 1956

On his trip to the United States June 8–15, 1956, Chancellor Adenauer gave the following address at the Yale University commencement exercises:

I look upon it as a great honor that Yale University today has awarded me the honorary degree of Doctor of Laws.

It is a great distinction to receive an honorary degree from Yale, in particular. I am especially happy to be able to speak at one of the most venerable abodes of American intellectual life.

Let me avail myself of this opportunity to thank your university for having cultivated—in pursuit of its noble ideal of education—the study of German letters even in a dark age. A number of scholars of German origin hold high academic degrees from your university; and the Goethe Collection of the Yale Library is considered one of the best, if not the best, outside Germany. It is, therefore, only an inadequate expression of our thanks that the German Federal Government has made available two scholarships for students of this university in the next academic year. We are glad to be able to receive your young compatriots as welcome guests in Germany and we hope that the exchange of young students, so fruitful for both sides, can be further encouraged in the future.

Ladies and gentlemen, you will now expect me to make some comments on the political situation as it appears to German eyes. Subject to the qualification that discussion of this broad subject within the compass of a short address is bound to remain sketchy, I would like to say this: It seems that we find ourselves at present in a new phase of the great conflict between East and West. The present leaders of the Soviet Union have pushed from his throne— after his death, it is to be noted—Stalin, the exponent of the policy of cruel hardship, of intimidation, of threat and violence. They have struck a fresh note.

It is undeniable that they are making an impression thereby on some people. We cannot tell with certainty the reasons which led them to disavow Stalinism, but one thing can be said with assurance: There are no signs to indicate that the disavowal of Stalinism means the acceptance of those spiritual principles which are the foundation of the free world. Instead, there are only new forms and methods used by a new, more dexterous leadership in the Kremlin in order to achieve the old objectives of the Bolshevik regime—the domination of the world by Communism—more surely and with fewer sacrifices.

All the free nations are faced here with a question of the utmost importance, with the question: Is an unarmed peace possible? For the German people this question has special significance. Because of their geographic situation they are neighbors of Soviet power. By the iron curtain they are cut into two parts. Consequently they are especially disposed, perhaps, to place their hopes in a change of Soviet policy which would achieve the redemption of seventeen million Germans of the Soviet Zone from enslavement. Therefore, they are particularly ready to welcome with pleasure any evidence of a genuine change of mind in the leadership of the Soviet Union. But our own experiences have been too bitter and we have seen too clearly the meaning of Communism, the methods it uses and the diabolic skill with which its propaganda operates not to react to the latest events in Moscow with the utmost skepticism.

One thing, I believe, is certain—and this was also clearly borne out by the 20th Party Congress in Moscow: The leaders of the Soviet Union continue to believe that capitalism is doomed to destruction, and their aim is to make Communism the dominant power in the world.

The theory of "peaceful co-existence" currently being advanced by them does not by any means signify that they are prepared to respect the ideology of the West or even its continued existence. As far as the Soviets are concerned, "peaceful co-existence"—which they had used advantageously before—is merely another tactical phase in their campaign to weaken the cohesion of the free world and to improve their own position. In line with their goal, they are addressing themselves at present chiefly to the Asian-African nations.

So far, I think, the men in the Kremlin still owe us proof that they are ready also in their policy towards the free nations to act in accordance with their repudiation of Stalin. So far we have heard words but not seen any deeds. We have not seen any significant corrections of the most flagrant manifestations of Stalin's imperialism. Even the allies of the Soviet Union are still denied those rights to which the Soviet Union, by signing the Charter of the United Nations, pledged itself. In this connection I recall to you Article Two, paragraph four, of the Charter and would ask you to compare the principles laid down there with the reality as it exists in Eastern and Central Europe.*

---

*The text of this paragraph of the Charter reads as follows: "All members shall refrain in their international relations from the threat or use of force against the territorial integrity or political independence of any state, or in any other manner inconsistent with the purposes of the United Nations."

The men in the Kremlin are still not prepared to remove the main causes of the tension in the world. They also refuse to make any real concessions on the German issue—for example. In fact with regard to the German issue, Mr. Khrushchev expressed himself more ruthlessly to French Premier Mollet and French Foreign Minister Pineau during their visit to Moscow when he stated that he would rather have 17 million Germans on his side than a re-united neutral Germany. Can you think of a more emphatic endorsement of brute force? I beg you, ladies and gentlemen, to consider the German question, the question of German reunification, not only as a German right but also as a question of natural law. The question of German reunification is the pivot on which European stability hinges and, consequently, world peace depends. Khrushchev quite evidently also sees it in that light.

Throughout the world the Soviets aggravate existing conflicts and endeavor to undermine the West's position in an unscrupulous manner. Their course seems clear to me: They want to lull the vigilance of the free world and to weaken its readiness to defend itself. Above all, however, they want to smash first the mighty protective shield of the North Atlantic Treaty Organization and to drive the United States from Europe so that Europe will fall like a ripe fruit into the Soviet lap and through its industrial potential and the skill of its people will lend the Soviets decisive superiority over the United States.

I consider the new tactics of the Soviet Union more dangerous than the former aggressive conduct, since it plays upon the longing for peace which lives in all men.

What, then, can the West do, what can we all do in this situation? I think it is the task of the responsible statesmen and of all the peoples of our free world to insure that the Soviet scheme does not succeed. First this requires one thing: We must on no account relax even one moment in our vigilance.

It is undeniable that recently the cohesion of the West has weakened and that there are clear indications of a lack of coordination in its foreign policy. Fortunately, the West possesses a great and strong organization which has so far deterred the Soviet Union from an attack. I refer to NATO, which was established at a time when the danger of a hot war existed. This danger is not at present acute, because the Kremlin hopes to achieve world domination through the slow undermining of the West. The new task is now to prevent this break-up of the West. For this purpose, too, NATO—further developed—is the proper instrument.

To my mind one cannot very well pursue an agreed military policy towards a nation without having, at the same time, maximum conformity in foreign policy aims in respect to that nation.

The West must not let the Soviets believe that while it does pursue a common military policy it is, on the other hand, possible for every single NATO member to pursue its own foreign policy—free from all restrictions—in relation to the Soviet Union. The mere impression that that is so must be avoided. The Soviet leaders live, after all, by the hope that the alliance of the free nations will, in the end, be torn by such deep dissensions as to let final success drop into the Soviet lap, as it were.

The utmost vigilance and justified distrust towards the policy of the Soviet Union does not, however, exclude the necessity for the West to be ready at all times to re-examine its policy to make sure it corresponds to developments in world policy. Thus, it is our duty to watch constantly for indications of a genuine change of mind and a genuine readiness to understand on the part of the countries behind the Iron Curtain. The path we are following in common has so far, in principle, proved to be correct. We must continue this path unwaveringly, and no Soviet smile, however enticing, should tempt us to relax in our common efforts before the Soviet side has shown concrete proof of a change of mind—especially with regard to its attitude to other nations oppressed by it.

An essential contribution towards the maintenance of peace must be made by the free nations of Europe. It cannot be denied that, as the immediate threat of war has receded in Europe, a selfish way of looking at national interests threatens to spread once more. In spite of this we can state that, through the work of the OEEC and of the coal and steel community, through the admission of the Federal Republic to NATO and through the establishment of the West European Union, a degree of political cooperation has been achieved in free Europe, from which point the work of the political unification of the old continent can be successfully carried on.

The concept that the states of Free Europe must join in a political and economic unit is a positive result of the last war. Many millions of Europeans, especially also in the Federal Republic of Germany, have been imbued with this idea and it is the guiding principle of the foreign policy of the German Federal Government. The freedom—the very existence of Europe—depends more than ever on Europe's ability to realize this concept. A disrupted and disunited Europe must sooner or later succumb to the power threatening the continent. Europe, however, can survive the difficult and protracted period of growing together only if the United States of America continues to maintain its strong protection of the old continent. It gave me great pleasure, therefore, that the United States recently demonstrated once again its readiness to do so and its undiminished interest in the creation of a united and free Europe. President Eisenhower told Baylor University in Texas on May 25th

14

that the United States was patient in this matter. I know how difficult this waiting must be for you as American citizens and what annoyance the Europeans' slowness must cause you. In spite of all the impatience which you might feel, may your great people always realize that by defending in Europe the moral and spiritual values of the West as a whole they are also defending themselves.

The Federal Republic of Germany is prepared to make every possible contribution towards the creation of a united Europe, and I think, when you study the years since 1949, you will find that we have, indeed, achieved quite a few things in this field. In this context a good relationship between Germany and France appears to us to be the nucleus of any European integration. Since the establishment of the Federal Republic we have worked with all our strength to improve this relationship, and our efforts are bearing fruit. For example, look at the way in which our two countries during the last few months have dealt dispassionately and constructively with the thorny question of the Saar.

I think I can say that without the European policy pursued by Germany and France this difficult problem could never have been mastered in the way it was. Negotiations with M. Mollet and M. Pineau at Luxembourg on June 4th have strengthened again my conviction of the power and the force of the European idea. The policy of European integration has put on an entirely new basis our relations with those of our neighbors who enjoy the blessing of freedom. With many of them we cooperate most intimately today in all kinds of European organizations—for the benefit of all of us. Although only eleven years have passed since the end of the last war, we are joined through a military defense alliance with several of our neighbors. Within the framework of the West European Union and NATO—this seems to me a fact of particular importance—we are linked for the first time in our history—through a partnership which is of the greatest value to us—to that European power with which you have special ties; with Britain! As a result of this policy, a great deal has been achieved in an amazingly short period to overcome old disputes and conflicts.

Let me add a few words on the question of Germany's reunification—better, on the question of the liberation of 17,000,000 Germans in the Eastern Zone. It is not only a question concerning the Germans, not only a question of right, not only a question of the obligation of the four victorious powers to bring about reunification in peace and freedom. In the course of the last few years' developments it has become a European question, a question of great importance in world politics.

The control of Germany by the Soviet Union, the exercise of Soviet influence on Germany would mean a shift of power in the world in favor of the Soviet Union which would threaten the whole world, and also you in the United States.

Unification remains a question of common concern—both to the German people and to the four powers who have undertaken to bring it about. We are most grateful to the western powers for the attitude which they have adopted on this question. They have stated again and again that reunification of Germany in freedom and liberty constitutes one of the most important elements of a genuine easing of tension and that the implementation of any general disarmament—in which they are most interested—is not conceivable without simultaneous progress towards reunification of Germany.

As regards the German attitude, it is clear: We shall stand by the obligations which we have assumed. In particular, this concerns also the German contribution to the defense of the free world. In spite of great psychological difficulties confronting us after two world wars with disastrous consequences for the German people and after complete demilitarization, the plans made by NATO and by the German Federal Government regarding the establishment of German forces will be carried out. The announcement of a reduction in the Soviet armed forces will have no repercussions on our defense efforts. Germany wants to be and will remain a reliable partner of the West.

I have referred to the necessity for the West to remain vigilant and not to relax in its defense efforts, although the conflict in which we find ourselves cannot be won by military means alone. This is the reason for my reference to the absolute need for strengthening the West's political cooperation with regard to the Soviet Union. The maintenance of the defensive strength of the West, however, is the first and most indispensable condition for the maintenance of peace and freedom in the world.

The German people in the West and the East are imbued with profound longing for this peace and this freedom. This German people does not want any political adventures in the East. The German Federal Government, therefore, will continue the straight course of its policy pursued so far which, I am sure, will bring us the reunification of Germany. For this the Federal Government and the German people need also in the future the confidence and trust of their allies.

President Griswold, ladies and gentlemen, allow me to end by assuring you of my firm conviction that in the struggle between totalitarian oppression and free self-determination of the peoples a vigilant and united West, upholding its spiritual and moral values, can never be defeated.

I thank you.

6

Chancellor Adenauer's Senate Address,
May 27, 1957

While in the United States May 23–30, 1957, Chancellor Adenauer had the opportunity on May 27, 1957, of outlining the principles of German foreign policy to the U.S. Senate:

Mr. President, members of the Senate, I am very grateful for the opportunity you have accorded me to speak before you. This opportunity is an honor for me and my country. I wish to use it to outline in a few words the general direction of our foreign policy.

I hope, in this way, to contribute to a clear understanding which is the basis of genuine trust. At the same time I hope to make clear how deeply related are the basic principles characterizing American policy and German policy.

The first principle, the guiding motive of our policy is freedom. There may be differences of opinion on the methods by which freedom may best be assured and preserved. Although the Government led by me may consider dangerous some of the foreign policy solutions advocated by other political parties and groups—there is no difference of opinion among Germans in the sincere desire for freedom. Since the Bundestag elections of 1949, it has been clearly demonstrated where the Federal Republic of Germany stands in the great worldwide conflict between freedom and slavery. This is the deeper meaning of the decision taken at the polls by the German people in 1949.

When the German people regained their statehood and once more were able to exercise their own free will, the world was split into two camps and the border separating the free world from the Communist orbit ran through the heart of our country, dividing our people. It separated ancient German territory from us, land from which currents of creative spiritual life have enriched our western civilization. The German people did not hesitate to make an unequivocal decision. Since the elections of 1953 there has not been a single Communist in our freely elected parliament. Two grievous experiences influenced the choice of the German people: the experience with a totalitarian dictatorship imposed on us during the National Socialist regime and the daily contact with the reality of communism in the form of a Communist dictatorship in the Soviet Zone of Germany. But the German people have expressed their will for freedom not only by the rejection of totalitarianism but by the positive decision to form as close an alliance as possible with the other free peoples of the world. There is no more emphatic manifestation of this will than the policy of European integration consistently endorsed by the great majority of the German people and their elected representatives—a policy which the Federal Republic has pursued since its inception.

The Federal Republic has participated in all the European organizations set up in recent years: the Council of Europe, OEEC, and the Coal and Steel Community. These integrated communities, the Coal and Steel Community and the communities of the Common Market and of Euratom, which we hope will soon come to life, are particularly characteristic because in these organs the Federal Republic renounces part of its national sovereignty in the interest of larger European communities. It reflects great credit on the foresighted ones among the drafters of our Constitution that we can state today that our basic law already contained a provision permitting the transfer of sovereignty by simple majority vote in Parliament. That was a great decision. It meant no less than a repudiation of the idea, no longer valid in a disintegrating world of European polities, that the sovereign national state is the ultimate and highest entity of political organization—an idea which has cost Europe so much blood and treasure. We are glad that the idea of a larger European patriotism has formed roots, particularly among our young people. Through the medium of these European organizations our alliance with the free world has become truly unbreakable.

Our second goal is peace. The horrible experiences of the recent World War have left their marks on the German people. The millions of dead, the horrors of total war in which the hinterland is no longer left untouched, the terrible destruction of our cities, the ruin of our economy, the collapse of the administrative structure—all this is still alive in the minds of the German people. But since peace—according to the famous dictum of the German philosopher Immanuel Kant—is not a natural condition among the peoples but the result of a conscious effort of man, our policy has seized on all possibilities open to it to secure peace. With the creation of the United Nations mankind took a tremendous stride forward toward securing peace and justice in the world. This objective has not been attained as yet, because the Soviets have paralyzed the security mechanism of the United Nations by innumerable vetoes. As a result, an effort had to be made to bring about this security by the establishment of organizations parallel and supplementing the United Nations. The Charter of the United Nations, in wise foresight, has shown a path toward this end by confirming the right of individual and collective self-defense. This path logically led to the foundation of the Atlantic Community. The Atlantic Community is an instrument of peace because it is designed to deter any aggressor. It achieves this aim by coordinating and developing the armed strength of the free West in such a way that any aggression becomes too big a risk for the aggressor. This consideration has caused the Federal Republic to become a member of the Atlantic Community. Militaristic tendencies are far removed from our purpose and aggressive intentions even more so. Since we consider all our endeavors in the military sphere solely as defense efforts, we follow all the discussions on measures to bring about controlled disarmament with lively and positive interest. If these efforts are combined with elimination of the causes of tension in the world they must, in the end, bring to the world the blessing it so ardently desires: the safeguarding of peace.

The third basic principle of our policy is unity. You know of the heavy and oppressive burden weighing upon us because many millions of Germans are forced, against all justice and moral principles, to live separated from us and under Communist terror. In order to understand this fully, one must realize that what is at stake here is not merely a border problem which can be discussed and settled among neighbors. We are faced here primarily with a human problem—the arbitrary manner in which a people is torn apart—parents separated from their children, unable to see them except under extreme difficulty and danger. Millions of people are forced to live under a regime of lawlessness, arbitrary rule, and slavery.

The German Republic will be incomplete as long as it is confined to the territory of the Federal Republic. Let us recall the circumstances under which the Federal Republic was founded. After the moral and material collapse into which the National Socialist regime led us, the victorious nations assumed supreme power in Germany. The three western occupation powers, faithful to the responsibility which they shouldered at the same time, and to their principles which were also the principles of the United Nations, proceeded to rebuild a German state on a democratic basis. The Soviet Union, on the other hand, misused its trusteeship and subjugated the Soviet occupied zone to a subservient, satellite regime of Communists—a regime which had the backing of only an infinitesimal percentage of the population as was demonstrated during the popular uprising of June 17, 1953. Thus it happened that the Soviet zone did not participate in the development which gradually transformed Germany from an object of foreign rule into a responsible subject in the community of nations governing itself in accordance with democratic principles.

Therefore, we demand reunion with 17 million fellow Germans—people who are as German as we are and as freedom loving as we are, and who are no less entitled than we are to determine their own political destiny; we demand from the fourth of the victorious powers only that which the other three in loyal fulfillment of the responsibility assumed by them when the German state collapsed, have long since conceded of their own free will. Thus, our demand is basically a democratic one, for the essence of democracy is to grant to a people regarding themselves as an entity that form of government which will permit them to live as a responsible member of the international community; and it is at the same time a requirement of any general policy aiming at the preservation of peace; for only the establishment of an all-German government would permit the conclusion of a peace treaty. This would endow Europe with that just and enduring political order which today— 12 years after the war—is still denied to it.

Political action is the art of bringing to life those concepts which have been recognized as the ethical foundation of justice. Freedom, peace, unity—these are the aims of our policy, a policy designed to give effect to the great ideals that determine the progress of humanity.

7

Chancellor Adenauer's Address to the U.S. House of Representatives, May 28, 1957

Chancellor Adenauer addressing the U.S. Congress, Washington, May 28, 1957. Behind the Chancellor: House Speaker Sam Rayburn.

In his speech to the U.S. House of Representatives, Dr. Adenauer outlined the development of the Federal Republic of Germany from its founding in 1949, and its political perspective:

Mr. Speaker, members of the House of Representatives:

I am deeply conscious of the honor of speaking before you, the elected representatives of the strongest and freest nation on earth; and with all my heart I thank you for this distinction. I know that I do not stand here for myself alone, but for all my countrymen. What I am going to say, therefore, is meant as a message from them to the great American people.

The Federal Republic of Germany is young—not quite eight years old. It is still incomplete and will remain incomplete as long as reunion with the seventeen million Germans living in the Soviet

21

Occupied Zone has not been effected. We have been sovereign for three years; only since then have we been the masters of our political decisions.

When totalitarian National Socialism collapsed, after having inflicted unspeakable suffering on the world and the German people, it left chaos behind. There were millions of dead and crippled, ten million people who were expelled from their ancestral homes in the German East, burned cities, industries and lines of transportation destroyed, the economy ruined, an administration functioning on an emergency basis only, desperate human beings and, above all, a younger generation dangerously exposed to pernicious nihilism.

The German people went to work, supported in their first steps by the Western occupation powers who gradually became our allies and friends. They reconstructed their homes, factories, stores, highways and railroads. The German people worked hard and with self-discipline. They received invaluable help from outside sources, both public and private, and especially from the American people. The great work of the Marshall Plan, undertaken ten years ago, will never be forgotten by Europeans. It is my heart-felt desire at this hour to express our gratitude for all of this.

Consciously and deliberately, rejecting all totalitarian thoughts and aims, we began to erect our Federal Republic in that part of Germany in which freedom and human rights could be reestablished; we created this Republic on the unshakable foundation of democracy—with the inspired words of Abraham Lincoln in mind—"Government of the people, by the people, for the people." Freedom, respect for the inalienable rights of the individual and the principle of the rule of law—this is the credo of our Constitution. In this respect, we could revert to the best traditions of our people. Our economy was organized on the princple of competitive free enterprise and social justice. We call this economic system the "Social Market Economy," and it combines free enterprise with social responsibility. The economic consequences of war destruction we endeavored to distribute equitably on many shoulders, in our thoroughgoing "Equalization of Burdens Law."

The greatest problems, however, were posed for us by the world around us, that is the international situation. The world of which our new Federal Republic had to become a part, was divided into two camps. This situation confronted our people with the most important decision it has ever had to make. Without hesitation we decided—and this is the meaning of the first parliamentary elections in 1949—for freedom against slavery, for the dignity of the individual against the collective mind, for rule by law against arbitrary dictatorship. Since 1953, there has not been a single Communist in our freely-elected parliament.

In repeated decisions of their own choice, the people of the Federal Republic by a large majority have confirmed that our nation constitutes an inseparable part of the free world. The basic expression of this attitude is our allegiance to the unit of Europe. Therefore, we became a member of the Strasbourg Council of Europe and the OEEC. We participated in the creation of the European Coal and Steel Community, in the attempt to create a European Defense Community and a European political community, and we hope that the Common Market and Euratom will soon be ratified by the parliaments of all six countries concerned. We have participated in all these works knowing that they mean an indissoluble bond to the world of freedom.

As early as 1948, when our Constitution was drafted by the Constituent Assembly—the Parliamentary Council under my presidency—we made a provision whereby parts of our sovereignty could be transferred by a simple law to a European community. This was a renunciation of the concept that national sovereignty is still a principle suitable to the establishment of a political order in Europe. This principle has cost Europe dearly in the many wars of the past.

With the free world we share the dangers which threaten it, dangers to peace. As a country whose very arteries are now cut—by the "Iron Curtain"—we are vividly aware of these dangers. Therefore, we need safeguards. We find these safeguards within the powerful North Atlantic Alliance whose main support is the moral, political, economic and military strength of the United States. NATO, in accordance with the principles of the United Nations, is an instrument for the preservation of freedom. The western world created it after the Soviets almost completely paralyzed the security mechanism of the United Nations which had been devised with so much care and idealism. In our strenuous efforts to make our contribution to the military strength of the alliance, we, too, have nothing else in mind but the defense of our liberty. On my word before God, nobody in Germany plays with the idea of using force or war, and this includes the use of force in the question of German reunification which we desire so ardently. Still fresh in our memory is the horror of the nights of bombing during the second World War, and the terrible devastation of our country.

That is why in our sincere love for peace we follow with such acute attention and sympathy the efforts of your Government by an overall controlled disarmament to diminish the danger of war. These efforts, coupled with elimination of the causes of tension in the world—characterized, most of all, in defiance of reason, justice and morality, by the division of my country and its courageous capitol, Berlin—must in the end give to mankind the security for which it longs and to which it is entitled in order to live according to its true destiny, to the highest principles of humanity. Without real effort, however, and without the sincere cooperation of the free peoples, we know that this objective will never be attained.

These are only the most essential facts and motives that may help you to understand us—that is, what we are and how we act. Let me attempt to sum up with a statement that gives me much pleasure:

The understanding and agreement—I daresay the cordial friendship—that exists today between the American and the German people is not the product of an accidental coincidence of transient interests. It rests on the common ground of profound convictions. It rests on the only power that moves free human beings to unite their destinies lastingly—it rests on confidence. The German people trust in you. Preserve your trust in them. This I ask of you.

8

Joint Declaration of May 28, 1957, Concerning the Discussions Between President Eisenhower and Chancellor Adenauer

In a joint declaration May 28, 1957, President Eisenhower and Chancellor Adenauer summarized their discussions as follows:

The President of the United States and the Chancellor of the Federal Republic of Germany concluded today the cordial discussions they have conducted during the last several days, with the assistance of the Secretary of State and the German Foreign Minister, and other advisers.

These discussions permitted a comprehensive exchange of views concerning German-United States relations, the European situation, and the world situation. They have served to strengthen still further the close understanding and harmony of views already existing between the two governments.

As a result of their talks, the President and the Chancellor have issued a Joint Declaration regarding matters of mutual interest.

Joint Declaration

I.

The President and the Chancellor agreed that the basic aim of the policies of their two countries is the maintenance of peace in freedom. To that end it is the common policy of their governments to work for the achievement of conditions in which all nations can live in peace and freedom and devote their energies and resources to promoting the welfare of their peoples.

They agreed that the realization of these conditions depends upon the removal of the causes of tension existing between the Soviet Union and the Free World. This tension is mainly attributable to the acts and policies of the Soviet Union, among them the deprivation of other peoples of their freedom.

The President and the Chancellor noted with great concern the consequences of the brutal Soviet intervention in Hungary. The continued suppression of the rights of the Hungarian people makes it difficult for other nations to accept as genuine the professed Soviet desires for peaceful coexistence.

The President and the Chancellor reaffirmed that the ending of the unnatural and unjust division of Germany is a major objective of the foreign policies of the two governments. Germany must be reunited on a free and democratic basis by peaceful means. If the Soviet rulers really desire peace and the relaxation of international tension, they can give no better proof than to permit the reunification of Germany through free elections.

The President and the Chancellor emphasized that the restoration of German national unity need give rise to no apprehension on the part of the Soviet Union as to its own security. It is not the purpose of their governments to gain any one-sided military advantage from the reunification of Germany. In conjunction with such reunification, they stand ready, as stated at the two Geneva conferences of 1955, to enter into European security arrangements which would provide far-reaching assurances to the Soviet Union.

II.

The President and the Chancellor agreed that NATO is essential for the protection of the security of the entire free world. They agreed that the defensive strength of NATO must be further improved in the face of the continuing Soviet threat and the absence of a dependable agreement for major reductions of armaments. The German Federal Government will proceed as rapidly as possible with building up its agreed contribution to the Western collective defense system.

For the purpose of contributing its fair share to the defense of the North Atlantic area, the United States intends to maintain forces in Europe, including Germany, as long as the threat to the area exists. As the North Atlantic Council agreed at its recent meeting at Bonn, the Atlantic Alliance must be in a position to use all available means to meet any attack which might be launched against it. The availability of the most modern weapons of defense will serve to discourage any attempt to launch such an attack.

III.

The President and the Chancellor expressed gratification over the significant progress made over the last several months toward closer economic integration in Europe. The Chancellor expressed his belief that the treaties establishing EURATOM and the European Common Market, signed at Rome on March 25 of this year, constitute a further step of historic significance toward European unity. The President expressed the great interest of the United States Government and of the American people in these treaties and his belief that their entry into force will benefit not only the people of Europe, but those of the entire world.

IV.

The two governments are in agreement that efforts must be pressed in the United Nations to reach agreement on measures for disarmament, with respect to both conventional and nuclear weapons, under an effective system of international control.

The President and the Chancellor agreed that, if a beginning could be made toward effective measures of disarmament, this would create a degree of confidence which would facilitate further progress in the field of disarmament and in the settlement of outstanding major political problems, such as the reunification of Germany.

They agreed that if such initial steps succeed they should be followed within a reasonable time by a comprehensive disarmament agreement which must necessarily presuppose a prior solution of the problem of German reunification. Accordingly, the Chancellor advised the President, as he has the French and British Governments, that the Federal Republic would consider that the conclusion of an initial disarmament agreement might be an appropriate time for a conference on the reunification of Germany among the Foreign Ministers of the four powers responsible therefor. The United States will consult with the French and British Governments regarding this matter.

The President stressed that any measures for disarmament applicable to Europe would be accepted by the United States only with the approval of the NATO allies, which he hoped would take a leading role in this regard, and taking into account the link between European security and German reunification. He assured the Chancellor that the United States does not intend to take any action in the field of disarmament which would prejudice the reunification of Germany. He stated that the United States would consult with the German Federal Government closely on all matters affecting Germany arising in the disarmament negotiations.

9

Welcoming Remarks by President Eisenhower
to President Heuss, June 5, 1958

President Eisenhower greeting President Heuss in Washington. At left, rear: Secretary of State John Foster Dulles.

Federal President Theodor Heuss visited the United States June 4–23, 1958. President Eisenhower's remarks at welcoming ceremonies in Washington June 4 refer to the fact that the event marks the first visit by a German head of state to the U.S.:

President Heuss and ladies and gentlemen:

Never before in history has the head of a German state visited this land. So it is with unusual warmth that I welcome you this morning to this Capital City and to this country.

In your lifetime and mine, Mr. President, the power of your nation and the power of this nation have been tragically plunged into war on opposite sides. The wounds of these wars seem to be, I think, almost wholly cured.

To today I think that the feeling of a friendship between the American people and the German people of the Federal German

28

Republic is the stronger, the more intense, because of the tribulations that we have been through and because of the way our two countries have met in peaceful conference, peaceful arrangements, to overcome those old memories and disasters.

And so I am sure that as you visit this country, you will discover that the American people reflect the same sentiments as I now give to you, which are: welcome here, very, very heartily.

10

Address by President Heuss Before the U.S. Congress, June 6, 1958

The address by Federal President Theodor Heuss before the U.S. Congress on June 6, 1958, dealt with Germany's past and with its present:

Mr. Speaker, Mr. President, members of the Congress of the United States, permit me first to make a personal remark.

I have chosen not without hesitation to address this august assembly in my own language. I would much rather have addressed the Congress of the United States in English—and have established thereby, perhaps, a more immediate communication with Members of both Houses. But I have come reluctantly to the conclusion that my command of your language is not what it used to be—that it has, in fact, become somewhat rusty. I must ask your indulgence, therefore, to allow me to speak to you in German.

I am grateful to President Eisenhower for his invitation because it gives me an opportunity to see for myself the reality of these United States. I think I know a little about this country's history. I know many of its citizens and I have had a great many discussions about the development and mentality of the people of this vast country. But already I feel that I shall not advance on my visit here beyond some very modest elementary lessons; and I, who have written a number of books, promise you that I shall not write a book as an expert on the United States when I return home. Nor do I want to compete with de Tocqueville. The dimensions to be grasped compel humility. But I do appreciate the honor of being able to address this distinguished assembly whose debates and acts today profoundly influence the world's destiny. It is a world responsibility which the American citizen has not sought but which he does not shirk.

I shall speak to you with the utmost candor. After Hitler's recklessness had forced the United States as well into his war, a shadow fell upon the American view of the German people: Every German seemed to be a Nazi. Today there is not much point in complaining about this distortion of the picture. After 1945 I said to many an officer of the occupation forces: You, who have never experienced the meanness and technical perfection of a totalitarian dictatorship, you are in the happy position in which you cannot even imagine the terrible moral pressure to which a people can be subjected. When we attempted, after 1945, to reestablish something

like public life on the basis of justice and democracy we, too, suffered much distress resulting from an outlook distorted by the
passions of war. After a time, however, we saw how the reality of
German life, little by little, was understood and interpreted.

Ten years ago I said that this was something quite new in
world history: Up to May 8, 1945, the American citizen had to pay
heavy taxes in order to destroy the German State whereas after
May 8 he had to pay taxes in order to save the German people. But
there was not merely the taxpayer's burden which after a few years
was absorbed into the grand design of the Marshall Plan which, in
turn, had evolved from the Hoover Report. In addition there was
the aid given by the individual American, by the churches, the
charitable organizations, by the countless and uncountable men
and women no matter whether they were of German origin or not.
The love of one's fellow man dissolved fear and hatred. I do not
come to you as a petitioner. I wish simply to express my gratitude
for the action which your Government has taken as well as for the
help rendered by millions of individual Americans. The material
side of this assistance was important but not decisive: It gave us
moral uplift and encouragement. Without the help of the United
States it would have been inconceivable for 10 million Germans
expelled from their homeland to be offered food, work and shelter.
The fact that week after week several thousand people flee to the
West from intellectual and spiritual slavery in the Soviet-occupied
zone continues to weigh heavy on the Federal Republic—their num-
bers have swelled to many hundreds of thousands. That stream of
human beings is at once a lasting grievance and a perpetual reproach.

I do not wish to take up the time at my disposal by discussing,
in terms of personalities, the German contribution to the growth
of American statehood and the development of the American way
of life. But I think I may say this much: The two great Presidents
of the United States, who have become legendary figures, come to
mind—George Washington knew that he could depend on the solid
work of organization done by the German General von Steuben
just as Abraham Lincoln could rely on the German champion of
freedom, Carl Schurz, the most prominent representative of the
many young Germans who came to the United States in quest of
those civic and political rights for which they had fought vainly in
Germany in 1848. The liberal and idealistic element represented
by those groups was easily integrated into the American historical
concept. And this concept was expanded and strengthened by the
tradition of diligent, skillful labor of the millions of people of German descent who have been absorbed—for which they are grateful,
I may say—into the substance of the American Nation.

31

We in Germany found ourselves in a strange situation after 1945. The people were exhuasted and starving; the attitude of many toward the victorious powers was "Do what you like with us." At that time the reproach was heard—also from this country—that the Germans were sorry for themselves. There was something in that. But with the coming of a sound currency and of the Marshall Plan, people in Germany saw that there was purpose again in hard work and effort. So the Germans set to work and put life into their economy again. In 1949 and 1950, I told prominent American businessmen frequently that the Marshall Plan funds were well-invested in Germany. Can you hold this against a people that they have regained economic strength through industriousness and skill, and thanks to the economic commonsense displayed by the United States which was the essential condition for German economic recovery? I find nothing more interesting than to read in some newspapers of the Western world—though not in the United States—that the Germans are once more becoming imperialists because they have more or less recovered their share of the world's market. Surely, there is no imperialism but much useful work in building sturdy cranes and manufacturing medical supplies.

During the past 50 years Germany has had the misfortune to acquire the reputation of being the nation which embodied, so to speak, eternal unrest and overweening ambition. A hundred years earlier—following the French revolution and the first Napoleon—other countries enjoyed this reputation. It would seem to me a good idea to get rid of such clichés encountered here and there in newspapers and schoolbooks.

We, all of us, must shed this habit of thinking, while, at the same time, not abandoning our traditional values. The German people—who here and there are still strangely suspected of exemplifying aggressive nationalism—existed as the Holy Roman Empire, as a European entity, imbued with a sense of responsibility toward Europe as a whole. And that was at a time when Spain, Britain, France, and later Russia, had long embarked upon a very concrete policy of expansion. I do not say this because I want to engage in polemics against historic events of bygone centuries—that is always a senseless thing to do—but in order to make the discussion about our present sitatuation a little easier.

It is remarkable: The Korean crisis—a scene of secondary importance in the traditional European concept of history—has laid open, both materially and psychologically, the fundamental issue—respect for law or for arbitrary power, for violent action or for free self-determination. I cannot here dwell on this. But I can say what the effect has been on us in Germany. National freedom—

including that aspect of it which concerns the social order—is a value which must be defended. It must be defended not only by those who are immediately affected but by all those to whom peace is a value per se and democracy a moral value. Believe me, it was not easy in Germany to explain the duty to military service to the man-in-the-street who had been persuaded by propaganda that his military service had been some sort of crime because the supreme command had been in the hands of criminals. And yet it was possible to establish in people's consciousness the natural feeling— that he who cherishes the security of his native soil and the maintenance of freedom must also help to safeguard them.

You must not expect of me a detailed exposition of our domestic German difficulties. National reunification not only remains the object of German longing but also the prerequisite for Europe's recovery. The slogan of coexistence may imply the coexistence of different ideologies in different national territories but it is absurd to base it on a relationship of total power on the one hand and total impotence on the other, which—look at the situation of 1945— disrupts a nation and denies it democratic self-determination.

The settlement of the Saar question has shown that a patient policy which recognizes democratic rights can lead to a happy result. An onerous burden has been lifted from German-French understanding, the cornerstone for strengthening an all-European consciousness. The German and the French people have equally contributed to this success and thereby have at long last brought about a good neighborly relationship between the two countries.

This much is evident: The Germans know where they belong. Their history, their intellectual and Christian-religious traditions have made them an integral part of what is called the Western World. On this point there can be no neutrality for us. There is something disquieting in the fear sometimes expressed in the Western press: Tomorrow they will reach an understanding with Soviet totalitarianism—that is what we term the "Rapallo complex"— or in the specter sometimes evoked in Germany: Washington and Moscow will come to an agreement and Germany will be the victim. It was very important to us—reassuring in a way—that President Eisenhower repeatedly made it very clear how much he felt Germany's tragic partition to be one of the heaviest mortgages on Europe's future. We shall never, never forget how President Truman by means of the so-called airlift in 1948–49, with the approval of the entire American people, saved Germany's old capital of Berlin— literally saved it—and thus decided the fate of Europe at a crucial point. The Germans, too, have perceived it as their duty to participate as free and active partners in the potentialities of peace and freedom implicit in this concept of the fate of Europe. Hence, the Federal Republic's loyal cooperation in the overall defense planning of NATO. Never again in the future shall German and American soldiers fight each other. And we realize that the sacrifice made by American mothers in having their sons in German garrisons—not, indeed, for the purpose of preparing wars but to prevent them by their presence and thereby to secure the democratic way of life for the future—we realize that this sacrifice corresponds to the great sense of duty which marks your tradition of liberty. And I am pleased to be able to state that, apart from a few unhappy incidents, many good, personal, and even, in some cases, family connections have developed, as well as much fruitful cooperation in the cultural and intellectual spheres.

It is not the case—as simple-minded people sometimes will have it—that it took two lost wars to force the Germans into the school of democracy. One of my pleasant memories is how a scholarly American officer in 1945 or 1946 explained to me that not only the Americans but also the Germans should know more about Germany's old democratic traditions which were preserved amidst the absolutism of the princes, and he gave me a lecture about the self-government of the old free and imperial cities of Germany. I have never forgtten this conversation, which struck a chord in my own family tradition. That was, indeed, a great German contribution to the evolving burgher civilization. And here, I suppose, is the point of contact and of mutual stimulation between the two sides. Behind us lie the bad times when the exchange of views and of knowledge was stopped. It is among the agreeable experiences of our time that people,through exchange visits, have been able to get to know one another; tens of thousands of Germans were able to absorb in this country the breath of your intellectual and political climate. And we on our part are glad to see the many Americans visiting our country once more—not only to see the romantic Rhine, which 100 or 50 years ago was the main attraction for travelers, but to acquaint themselves with our people, their achievements and their opinions.

I am coming to the end now, grateful that you have listened to me with patience. Believe me that our Germany will never again depart from the path of democracy and freedom. It is our sincere resolve to be good and dependable allies. As an institution the office of the German Federal President cannot be compared to that of the President of the United States. I would ask all those to appreciate this who expect declarations about such technical matters as the conclusion of a European security pact, methods of disarmament, and other problems. What we must aim at is to ease the social, economic, military, and political problems causing tension in the world—problems which have always existed but which have been aggravated since 1914. I have no illusions; I know that the pressing questions of giving substance to European political and economic cooperation, of achieving enduring settlement in the Near East, of safeguarding the free world against all dangers—that these are not to be minimized. These issues are full of difficulties, but examples have shown us that they are capable of solution; one need only recall the problems of Trieste and the Saar. It is my firm conviction that the peoples of the free world—deeply rooted as they are in the Christian faith—possess the moral strength to maintain their position and uphold their ideals. All that is required is to set in motion some of the all-pervasive forces inherent in human nature: reason, a sense of proportion, and perhaps a little love.

11

Joint Statement on the Occasion of President Eisenhower's Visit of August 27, 1958

On August 26–27, 1958, President Eisenhower visited Bonn. The following joint statement was issued following the discussions between Chancellor Adenauer and President Eisenhower:

The president of the United States visited the German Federal Capital on August 26 and 27, in order to confer with the German Federal Government. On the morning of August 27, President Eisenhower called on Federal President Heuss.

President Eisenhower and Chancellor Dr. Adenauer then had a private detailed discussion on world-wide political questions. Following this meeting, a larger meeting took place, including the President and the Chancellor and also the U.S. Secretary of State and the German Federal Minister of Foreign Affairs, as well as advisers of both governments. The discussions were conducted in the spirit of frankness and friendship characterizing the close ties between the two countries.

The President and the Chancellor discussed disarmament, the problems of Berlin and German reunification, European integration, and the continued cooperation of the two countries in the Atlantic Alliance. They reviewed in detail the results of the recent Geneva Conference. In this context Western policy in relation to the Soviet Union was discussed.

President Eisenhower and Chancellor Adenauer restated their belief that pacts of collective defense in accordance with Article 51 of the United Nations Charter contribute to the maintenance of world peace. The mutual cooperation of both their countries within the Atlantic Alliance, which alliance is of utmost importance to world peace, will therefore continue to be one of the pillars of the foreign policies of the two countries.

The President and the Chancellor reaffirmed their resolve to continue their efforts to achieve a just and peaceful solution of the problem of the tragic divison of Germany, a solution consistent with the desire of the German people and assuring peace and security in Europe. In this context President Eisenhower referred once again to the pledge given by the United States and its allies to protect the freedom and welfare of the people of Berlin.

12

Joint Communiqué After the Meeting Between President Kennedy and Chancellor Adenauer, November 22, 1961

Meeting between Chancellor Adenauer and President Kennedy at the White House, Washington, November 22, 1961.

Chancellor Adenauer and President Kennedy conferred in Washington on November 20–22, 1962. The communiqué issued following their discussions reflects East-West tensions, particularly in reference to Berlin:

The President and the Chancellor have had an extended exchange of views during the last three days on a number of problems of vital concern to their Governments. These exchanges took place in a frank and cordial atmosphere and established that there is substantial unanimity of view both on the substance of the problems and how to deal with them.

    The visit of the Chancellor afforded an opportunity to the foreign ministers and the defense ministers of the two countries to participate in the discussion and exchange views among themselves.

Berlin, over which the Soviet Union has created an international crisis, was the subject of earnest consultation. The President and the Chancellor reaffirmed their clear determination to insure the continuance of a free and vigorous life for the population of Berlin. They are in accord on the basic elements which will permit a peaceful resolution of this crisis through negotiation if there is reasonableness on the part of the Soviet Union. They agreed on the measures which should be taken in pursuing this objective in a manner consistent with the legitimate interests of all parties concerned. At the same time they also agreed on the necessity for maintaining and increasing the ability of the NATO alliance to cope with any military developments. These discussions will be continued through the already announced meetings between Chancellor Adenauer, Prime Minister Macmillan and President de Gaulle and concluded in the foreign ministers' meeting and the NATO Ministerial meeting scheduled in mid-December in Paris.

The President and the Chancellor reaffirmed the ultimate goal of their Governments of achieving by peaceful means the reunification of Germany on the basis of self-determination. They were also in agreement that this objective could be realized without prejudice to the legitimate interests of the Soviet Union and Germany's neighbors.

The President and the Chancellor reviewed the state of the North Atlantic Treaty Organization. They welcomed the measures now in progress to strengthen the alliance, but recognized the need for a sustained effort to further improve the ability of the alliance to resist aggression.

The President and the Chancellor noted Soviet charges accusing the NATO alliance of aggressive intent, and singling out the Federal Republic of Germany and its democratically elected Government as the principal object of its false and unwarranted attack. In this regard, the President and the Chancellor reaffirmed that:

(1) The North Atlantic alliance is an alliance for defense against aggression which abides fully by the requirements of the Charter of the United Nations. The peaceful characteristics of its members and their freedom from coercion make it manifestly impossible for NATO to commit aggression against anyone.

(2) The Federal Republic of Germany has demonstrated that it looks to its legitimate security interests entirely with the North Atlantic alliance, and to this end has integrated its entire effective defense establishment into the multinational NATO framework. The Chancellor, in emphasizing the defensive aspects of West German armed forces, noted that the Federal Republic is the only nation of its size all of whose forces are under international command.

While agreeing on the need to take all measures essential to strengthen the defensive posture of NATO, the President and the Chancellor recognized the necessity of not permitting Soviet pressure over Berlin to deflect them from urgently required constructive tasks vital to the welfare of their peoples and those of other nations.

The President reaffirmed the strong support of the United States for the movement toward European unity through the European Economic Community, the European Coal and Steel Community, and Euratom. The President and the Chancellor agreed on the important role that the development of the European communities can play in further strengthening and complementing the entire Atlantic community. They agreed particularly on the importance and significance of proposals now being considered for a European political union pursuant to the Bonn declaration of July, 1961.

They welcomed the recent decisions by the O. E. C. D. Council of Ministers to increase the combined gross national product of the O. E. C. D. member countries by 50 per cent in 1970 and pledged themselves to work toward this goal.

The President and the Chancellor also discussed the urgent need to increase the flow of development assistance to the less-developed countries. They noted that the Development Assistance Committee of the O. E. C. D. provides an excellent means of stimulating a greater effort in this field. They considered that in many cases the application of combined resources from several capital-exporting countries to specific development assistance problems would be a valuable method of assisting the less-developed countries.

It is the view of the President and the Chancellor that the fruitful exchange of views which they have had will facilitate the close cooperation between the United States and the Federal Republic and result in further strengthening the ties of friendship and mutual understanding which have characterized their relations in the post-war period.

13

Remarks by Chancellor Adenauer and President Kennedy at Welcoming Ceremonies in Bonn, June 23, 1963

President Kennedy paid an official visit to the Federal Republic of Germany June 23–26, 1963. Upon Mr. Kennedy's arrival, Chancellor Adenauer and the President characterized the status of German-American relations as follows:

The Chancellor. Mr. President:

It is with great pleasure that I welcome you here, Mr. President, and your party, in the Federal Republic of Germany. Your visit is most particularly appreciated by us, since it is a mark of the deep friendship which has bound the German and the American peoples together for many years. Your visit, Mr. President, is a political act.

On the 10th of June, you stated before the American University in Washington that the United States of America stood by its commitment to defend Western Europe and West Berlin. In the same speech, you said, Mr. President, that the United States would make no deal with the Soviet Union at the expense of other nations, and other peoples. You said, too, Mr. President, that not only did America's interests converge with those of its allies, but that there was also an identity of purpose and objectives, namely, the defense of freedom and the search for peace.

Could there have been any better way for you to demonstrate such determination than by visiting the Federal Republic and other countries in Western Europe, than by paying a visit to Berlin? We thank you, Mr. President, for coming here. You could not have done anything more effective to strengthen the cohesion within the Alliance. During your visit you will see various towns and districts of Germany, and wherever you go—and I am sure you have felt it already on your arrival and the reception given to you here at this airfield—wherever you go you will become aware of the feelings of gratitude and friendship the Germans have for the American people. I welcome you once again, Mr. President, from the bottom of my heart.

Thank you.

The President. Mr. Chancellor, Ministers:

I am grateful for your invitation and I am happy to be here. I have crossed the Atlantic, some 3,500 miles, at a crucial time in the life of the Grand Alliance. Our unity was forged in a time of danger; it must be maintained in a time of peace. Our Alliance was founded to deter a new war; it must now find the way to a new peace. Our strategy was born in a divided Europe, but it must look to the goal of European unity and an end to the divisions of people and countries. Our Alliance is in a period of transition, and that is as it should be. Western Europe is no longer weakened by conflict, but is fast becoming a full partner in prosperity and security. Western Europe is no longer the seedbed of world war, but an instrument of unity and an example of reconciliation. And Western Europe, finally, is no longer an area of assistance, but can now be a source of strength to all the forces of freedom all around the globe. I have also come to this country, the most populous in Western Europe, to express the respect of the people of the United States for the German peoples' industry and their initiative, for their culture and their courage.

Here in Western Germany you have achieved a solid framework of freedom, a miracle of economic recovery, and an opportunity to express your political ideals through action in Europe and throughout the world.

The people of West Germany have freed themselves from the forces of tyranny and aggression. The people of the United States have now freed themselves from the long process of isolation. Together we look forward to a new future. Former foes have become faithful friends. Nations bitterly arrayed against each other have now become closely allied, sharing common values and common sentiments, as well as common interests, working within a growing partnership of equals for peace and the common defense on problems of trade and monetary policy, and on helping the less developed countries, and on building Western unity. Above all, we recognize a duty to defend and to develop the long Western tradition which we share, resting as it does on a common heritage. Economically, militarily, politically, our two nations and all the other nations of the Alliance are now dependent upon one another. We are allies in the only war we seek—the war against poverty, hunger, disease, and ignorance in our own countries, and around the world.

We all know the meaning of freedom and our people are determined upon its peaceful survival and success.

My stay in this country will be all too brief, but in a larger sense the United States is here on this continent to stay. So long as our presence is desired and required, our forces and commitments will remain. For your safety is our safety, your liberty is our liberty, and any attack on your soil is an attack upon our own. Out of necessity, as well as sentiment, in our approach to peace as well as war, our fortunes are one.

Finally, I have also come to Germany to pay tribute to a great European statesman, an architect of unity, a champion of liberty, a friend of the American people—Chancellor Konrad Adenauer. Already he lives in the history he helped to make. I look forward to this visit with Chancellor Adenauer with me, and with the warmth of your greeting already in my memory.

14

Toasts by President Kennedy and Chancellor Adenauer at a Dinner on June 24, 1963

At a dinner given at the American Embassy Club in Bad Godesberg June 24, 1963, President Kennedy and Chancellor Adenauer gave the following toasts:

The President.

I know that all of us who have come from the United States have been very much warmed, heartened, encouraged, strengthened by the generosity of the reception we have received from all of you and from the people of the Federal Republic. I don't think that there is any substitute, however reliable and however much we admire the press, for an opportunity to visit firsthand and see the American people as the Chancellor has done, than for us to see the German people. Everything else falls away against this opportunity to come face to face, so that while the Chancellor and many of us will be meeting on Wednesday in Berlin, I do want to take this opportunity to express our warm appreciation to all of you, the strong feeling of confidence it has given us.

I think it renewed the life, although it didn't really need that, of our relationship, and in every way we have been made extremely happy by our visit. We are very much indebted to you all and we are most indebted to the people whom you serve.

I want to express my special appreciation to the Chancellor. As I said yesterday, he made, as did my predecessors in the United States, the crucial and the correct judgment. I think that he has been generous enough to say that perhaps the United States was the only one that made the long, right judgment in the late forties and in the fifties, and he on his part, and all of you as colleagues, also made the right judgment. And that will entitle my predecessors and will entitle the Chancellor and those who have worked with him, it seems to me, to a very important page in the history of our times, which is going to be recorded, I think, as the most significant times of the last years, in fact, the last centuries. These are the critical days because whether the world survives or not is a matter that comes before us for judgment, at least once every year, and I suppose it is going to go on that rather doleful path. But the Chancellor in his time, meeting his responsibility, made the right judgment and, therefore, he is an historic figure and one to whom all of

43

us who believe so strongly in the cause of freedom feel privileged to come and pay him our high esteem.

I hope that all of you will join in drinking with me to a distinguished leader of your country and also a distinguished leader of the West, the Chancellor.

The Chancellor. Mr. President, gentlemen:

I am deeply touched by what President Kennedy has just said. I am deeply moved because in my opinion it was the United States, at first Mr. Acheson and Mr. Truman, then Mr. Dulles and President Eisenhower, who have helped us Germans, a conquered people, who were completely down at the time.

I don't particularly like to make such acknowledgments, but let us face it; historic honesty requires that we say that the war which destroyed Germany was provoked by Germany; that the United States has shown the great vision to help the defeated enemy, which was really a deed which is only very rarely found in history.

You, Mr. President, have been here since yesterday. All of us, since your arrival at the airport, have had so many impressions, so many deeply moving experiences—this is certainly true for me—that we can say that a real epoch has been characterized by this visit. You saw yesterday, as we all did, and you have heard the masses in the squares, and you have seen in their eyes the real gratitude which they wanted to express. Now, gratitude is a very rare virtue, and certainly it is particularly rare in politics, but you have seen it directly with your own eyes, that these masses of people who lined the streets in Cologne, in the cathedral, in Bonn, in the Market Square, were filled with a real desire to demonstrate to you, as the representative of the United States, how grateful they are for everything that the United States has done, particularly for us Germans. I feel that these impressions may, in the difficult moments which you will face in the future, at a time when you will have to make more decisions, help you a little. And if these impressions at the time you have to make such decisions will be revived in front of you, then they may help you make the decisions with that clarity and that forcefulness whch statesmen require. If we can make a little contribution in this sense, I think that would be the best result of your visit here.

I want to thank you in the name of all of us Germans for coming here, and I want to emphasize between the United States and us, after all that is behind us, no split or separation, or whatever you want to call it, will ever happen again. We realize that the leadership is yours, not only because of your great nuclear strength,

44

but because of the great political acumen and the moral strength which you and your country have shown. It is, let me say it again, you, as the victors, gave your hand to us as the vanquished, that this is something which I think is the finest that any people can do.

May the memories of these days of your visit to Germany remain alive and may the thanks of the thousands contribute a little to help you make decisions in the same spirit which the United States has shown in the past, and which forever has insured for the United States a golden page in history. I propose a toast in honor of the President of the United States.

15

Joint Communiqué of June 24, 1963

The following joint communiqué was issued June 24, 1963, in Bonn following the discussions between President Kennedy and Chancellor Adenauer:

The President of the United States of America, John F. Kennedy, visited Bonn on June 23 and 24 and held talks with leaders of the Federal Republic of Germany. He had a private visit with Federal President Lübke, and on June 24 met privately with Chancellor Adenauer for detailed discussions on the general international situation. The President and the Chancellor were later joined by Secretary of State Rusk, Vice-Chancellor Erhard and the Federal Minister of Foreign Affairs, Schröder, as well as other officials and advisers of the two Governments.

President Kennedy and Chancellor Adenauer discussed European integration, relations between the European Community and other nations of Europe, progress toward the achievement of the Atlantic partnership, and the problems of Berlin and German reunification. In this connection, they had an exchange of views on Western policy toward the Soviet Union and the countries of Eastern Europe.

The President and the Chancellor were in agreement that the two Governments would continue their close collaboration in the task of developing genuine unity among the nations of Europe and fostering an integrated European Community in close partnership with the United States. On questions of economics and trade, both in their multilateral and bilateral aspects, the President and the Chancellor reaffirmed their agreement on basic aims, among these matters they stressed in particular the need for stronger participation in world trade by the developing countries. They agreed that the strength of the Free World rests in common policies and common aims pursued jointly by all the nations dedicated to establishing peace in freedom.

The Federal Government shares the view of the United States and other allied powers that controlled disarmament and agreement on the cessation of atomic weapons tests would constitute an important step toward the avoidance of a dangerous armaments race.

The exchange of views confirmed full agreement on the principle that the North Atlantic Alliance continues to be a major instrument for the maintenance of freedom, and the President and the Chancellor agreed that every effort will be made to strengthen common defense planning and joint operation of NATO defense forces.

The President and the Chancellor discussed the proposed multilateral seaborne MRBM force. The multilateral organization is considered a good instrument for serving all members of the Alliance in combining their defense efforts. They reaffirmed their agreement to use their best efforts to bring such a force into being. They also agreed that discussions about the principal questions involved in the establishment of such a force should be pursued with other interested Governments.

They reaffirmed the commitment of their two Governments to the right of self-determination, as embodied in the United Nations Charter, and to the achievement of German reunification in peace and freedom. They agreed that the freedom of Berlin will be preserved by every necessary means, and that the two Governments would seek every opportunity to counter the inhuman effects of the Wall. They also agreed that the two Governments would continue to seek to reduce tension through international understanding.

Peace and freedom are prerequisites for overcoming the obstacles that still prevent the greater part of mankind from enjoying full participation in social and economic development. The President and the Chancellor affirmed that the Governments of the United States and the Federal Republic of Germany are determined to assume their part in these tasks in the context of the free world's strategy of peace.

The discussions took place in spirit of frankness and cordiality. These meetings have shown full agreement between the two Governments in assessing the international situation, and have once again demonstrated the close and friendly relations which exist between the two countries.

16

Speech by President Kennedy in the
Paulskirche in Frankfurt, June 25, 1963

On June 25, 1963, President Kennedy gave a speech in the Paulskirche in Frankfurt, to representatives of German political life. In his introductory remarks, President Kennedy referred to the significance of the 1848 Paulskirche parliament for the democratic development of Germany:

I am most honored, Mr. President, to be able to speak in this city before this audience, for in this hall I am able to address myself to those who lead and serve all segments of a democratic system, Mayors, Governors, Members of Cabinets, civil servants, and concerned citizens. As one who has known the satisfaction of the legislator's life, I am particularly pleased that so many Members of your Bundestag and Bundesrat are present today, for the vitality of your legislature has been a major factor in your demonstration of a working democracy, a democracy worldwide in its influence. In your company also are several of the authors of the Federal Constitution who have been able through their own political service to give a new and lasting validity to the aims of the Frankfurt Assembly.

One hundred and fifteen years ago a most learned parliament was convened in this historic hall. Its goal was a united German federation. Its members were poets and professors, lawyers and philosophers, doctors and clergymen, freely elected in all parts of the land. No nation applauded its endeavors as warmly as my own. No assembly ever strove more ardently to put perfection into practice. And though in the end it failed, no other building in Germany deserves more the title of "cradle of German democracy."

But can there be such a title? In my own home city of Boston, Faneuil Hall—once the meeting place of the authors of the American Revolution—has long been known as the "cradle of American liberty." But when, in 1852, the Hungarian patriot Kossuth addressed an audience there, he criticized its name. "It is," he said, "a great name—but there is something in it which saddens my heart. You should not say 'American liberty'. You should say 'liberty in America'. Liberty should not be either American or European—it should just be 'liberty'."

Kossuth was right. For unless liberty flourishes in all lands, it cannot flourish in one. Conceived in one hall, it must be carried out in many. Thus the seeds of the American Revolution had been brought earlier from Europe, and they later took root around the world. And the German Revolution of 1848 transmitted ideas and idealists to America and to other lands. Today, in 1963, democracy and liberty are more international than ever before. And the spirit of the Frankfurt Assembly, like the spirit of Faneuil Hall, must live in many hearts and nations if it is to live at all.

For we live in an age of interdependence as well as independence—an age of internationalism as well as nationalism. In 1848 many countries were indifferent to the goals of the Frankfurt Assembly. It was, they said, a German problem. Today there are no exclusively German problems, or American problems, or even European problems. There are world problems—and our two countries and continents are inextricably bound together in the tasks of peace as well as war.

We are partners for peace—not in a narrow bilateral context but in a framework of Atlantic partnership. The ocean divides us less than the Mediterranean divided the ancient world of Greece and Rome. Our Constitution is old and yours is young, and our culture is young and yours is old, but in our commitment we can and must speak and act with but one voice. Our roles are distinct but complementary—and our goals are the same: peace and freedom for all men, for all time, in a world of abundance, in a world of justice.

That is why our nations are working together to strengthen NATO, to expand trade, to assist the developing countries, to aline our monetary policies, and to build the Atlantic community.

I would not diminish the miracle of West Germany's economic achievement. But the true German miracle has been your rejection of the past for the future—your reconciliation with France, your participation in the building of Europe, your leading role in NATO, and your growing support for constructive undertakings throughout the world.

Your economic institutions, your constitutional guarantees, your confidence in civilian authority, are all harmonious to the ideals of older democracies. And they form a firm pillar of the democratic European community.

But Goethe tells us in his greatest poem that Faust lost the liberty of his soul when he said to the passing moment: "Stay, thou art so fair." And our liberty, too, is endangered if we pause for the passing moment, if we rest on our achievements, if we resist the pace of progress. For time and the world do not stand still. Change is the law of life. And those who look only to the past or the present are certain to miss the future.

The future of the West lies in Atlantic partnership—a system of cooperation, interdependence, and harmony whose peoples can jointly meet their burdens and opportunities throughout the world. Some say this is only a dream, but I do not agree. A generation of achievement—the Marshall Plan, NATO, the Schuman Plan, and the Common Market—urges us up the path to greater unity.

There will be difficulties and delays. There will be doubts and discouragement. There will be differences of approach and opinion. But we have the will and the means to serve three related goals—the heritage of our countries, the unity of our continents and the interdependence of the Western Alliance.

Some say that the United States will neither hold to these purposes nor abide by its pledges—that we will revert to a narrow nationalism. But such doubts fly in the face of history. For 18 years the United States has stood its watch for freedom all around the globe. The firmness of American will and the effectiveness of American strength have been shown, in support of free men and free governments, in Asia, in Africa, in the Americas, and, above all, here in Europe. We have undertaken, and sustained in honor, relations of mutual trust and obligation with more than 40 allies. We are proud of this record, which more than answers doubts. But in addition these proven commitments to the common freedom and safety are assured, in the future as in the past, by one great fundamental fact—that they are deeply rooted in America's own self-interest. Our commitment to Europe is indispensable—in our interest as well as yours.

It is not in our interest to try to dominate the European councils of decision. If that were our objective, we would prefer to see Europe divided and weak, enabling the United States to deal with each fragment individually. Instead we have and now look forward to a Europe united and strong—speaking with a common voice, acting with a common will—a world power capable of meeting world problems as a full and equal partner.

This is in the interest of us all. For war in Europe, as we learned twice in 40 years, destroys peace in America. A threat to the freedom of Europe is a threat to the freedom of America. That is why no administration—no administration—in Washington can fail to respond to such a threat—not merely from good will but from necessity. And that is why we look forward to a united Europe in an Atlantic partnership—an entity of interdependent parts, sharing equally both burdens and decisions, and linked together in the tasks of defense as well as the arts of peace.

This is no fantasy. It will be achieved by concrete steps to solve the problems that face us all: Military, economic and political.

Partnership is not a posture but a process, a continuous process that grows stronger each year as we devote ourselves to common tasks.

The first task of the Atlantic community was to assure its common defense. That defense was and still is indivisible. The United States will risk its cities to defend yours because we need your freedom to protect ours. Hundreds of thousands of our soldiers serve with yours on this continent, as tangible evidence of that pledge. Those who would doubt our pledge or deny this indivisibility—those who would separate Europe from America or split one ally from another—would only give aid and comfort to the men who make themselves our adversaries and welcome any Western disarray.

The purpose of our common military effort is not war but peace, not the destruction of nations but the protection of freedom. The forces that West Germany contributes to this effort are second to none among the Western European nations. Your nation is in the frontline of defense, and your divisions, side by side with our own, are a source of strength to us all.

These conventional forces are essential, and they are backed by the sanction of thousands of the most modern weapons here on European soil and thousands more, only minutes away, in posts around the world. Together our nations have developed for the forward defense of free Europe a deterrent far surpassing the present or prospective force of any hostile power.

Nevertheless it is natural that America's nuclear position has raised questions within the alliance. I believe we must confront these questions, not by turning the clock backward to separate nuclear deterrents, but by developing a more closely unified Atlantic deterrent, with genuine European participation.

How this can best be done, and it is not easy—in some ways more difficult than to split the atom physically—how this can best be done is now under discussion with those who may wish to join in this effort. The proposal before us is for a new Atlantic force. Such a force would bring strength instead of weakness, cohesion instead of division. It would belong to all members, not one, with all participating on a basis of full equality. And as Europe moves toward unity, its role and responsibility, here as elsewhere, would and must increase accordingly.

Meanwhile there is much to do. We must work more closely together on strategy, training, and planning. European officers from NATO are being assigned to Strategic Air Command headquarters in Omaha, Nebraska. Modern weapons are being deployed here in Western Europe. And America's strategic deterrent, the most powerful in history, will continue to be at the service of the whole alliance.

Second: Our partnership is not military alone. Economic unity is also imperative, not only among the nations of Europe but across the wide Atlantic. Indeed, economic cooperation is needed throughout the entire free world. By opening our markets to the developing countries of Africa, Asia, and Latin America, by contributing our capital and our skills, by stabilizing basic prices, we can help assure them of a favorable climate for freedom and growth. This is an Atlantic responsibility. For the Atlantic nations themselves helped to awaken these peoples. Our merchants and traders ploughed up their soils—and their societies as well—in search of minerals and oil and rubber and coffee. Now we must help them gain full membership in the 20th century, closing the gap between rich and poor.

Another great economic challenge is the coming round of trade negotiations. Those deliberations are much more important than a technical discussion of trade and commerce. They are an opportunity to build common industrial and agricultural policies across the Atlantic. They are an opportunity to open up new sources of demand to give new impetus to growth, and make more jobs and prosperity, for our expanding populations. They are an opportunity to recognize the trading needs and aspirations of other free-world countries, including Japan.

In short, these negotiations are a test of our unity. While each nation must naturally look out for its own interests, each nation must also look out for the common interest—the need for greater markets on both sides of the Atlantic, the need to reduce the imbalance between developed and underdeveloped nations—and the need to stimulate the Atlantic economy to higher levels of production rather than to stifle it by higher levels of protection.

We must not return to the 1930's, when we exported to each other our own stagnation. We must not return to the discredited view that trade favors some nations at the expense of others. Let no one think that the United States, with only a fraction of its economy dependent on trade and only a small part of that with Western Europe, is seeking trade expansion in order to dump our goods on this continent. Trade expansion will help us all.

The experience of the Common Market, like the experience of the German Zollverein, shows an increased rise in business activity and general prosperity resulting for all participants in such trade agreements, with no member profiting at the expense of another. As they say on my own Cape Cod, a rising tide lifts all the boats. And a partnership, by definition, serves both partners, without domination or unfair advantage. Together we have been partners in adversity; let us also be partners in prosperity.

Beyond development and trade is monetary policy. Here again our interests run together. Indeed there is no field in which the wider interest of all more clearly outweighs the narrow interest of one. We have lived by that principle, as bankers of freedom, for a generation. Now that other nations, including West Germany, have found new economic strength, it is time for common efforts here, too. The great free nations of the world must take control of our monetary problems if those problems are not to take control of us.

Third and finally, our partnership depends on common political purpose. Against the hazards of division and lassitude, no lesser force will serve. History tells us that disunity and relaxation are the great internal dangers of an alliance. Thucydides reported that the Peloponnesians and their allies were mighty in battle but handicapped by their policymaking body—in which, he related "each presses it own ends ... which generally results in no action at all ... they devote more time to the prosecution of their own purposes than to the consideration of the general welfare—each supposes that no harm will come of his own neglect, that it is the business of another to do this or that—and so, as each separately entertains the same illusion, the common cause imperceptibly decays."

Is that also to be the story of the Grand Alliance? Welded in a moment of imminent danger, will it disintegrate in complacency, with each member pressing its own ends to the neglect of the common cause? This must not be the case. Our old dangers are not gone beyond return, and any division among us would bring them back in doubled strength.

Our defenses are now strong, but they must be made stronger. Our economic goals are now clear, but we must get on with their performance. And the greatest of our necessities, the most notable of our omissions, is progress toward unity of political purpose.

For we live in a world in which our own united strength and will must be our first reliance. As I have said before, and will say again, we work toward the day when there may be real peace between us and the Communists. We will not be second in that effort. But that day is not yet here.

We in the United States and Canada are 200 million, and here on the European side of the Atlantic alliance are nearly 300 million more. The strength and unity of this half billion human beings are and will continue to be the anchor of all freedom, for all nations. Let us from time to time pledge ourselves again to the common purposes. But let us go on, from words to actions, to intensify our efforts for still greater unity among us, to build new associations and institutions on those already established. Lofty words cannot construct an alliance or maintain it; only concrete deeds can do that.

The great present task of construction is here on this continent, where the effort for a unified free Europe is under way. It is not for Americans to prescribe to Europeans how this effort should be carried forward. Nor do I believe that there is any one right course or any single final pattern. It is Europeans who are building Europe.

Yet the reunion of Europe, as Europeans shape it—bringing a permanent end to the civil wars that have repeatedly wracked the world—will continue to have the determined support of the United States. For that reunion is a necessary step in strengthening the community of freedom. It would strengthen our alliance for its defense. And it would be in our national interest as well as yours.

It is only a fully cohesive Europe that can protect us all against fragmentation of the alliance. Only such a Europe will permit full reciprocity of treatment across the ocean, in facing the Atlantic agenda. With only such a Europe can we have a full give-and-take between equals, an equal sharing of responsibilities, and an equal level of sacrifice. I repeat again—so that there may be no misunderstanding—the choice of paths to the unit of Europe is a choice which Europe must make. But as you continue this great effort, undeterred by either difficulty or delay, you should know that this new European greatness will be not an object of fear but a source of strength for the United States of America.

There are other political tasks before us. We must all learn to practice more completely the art of consultation on matters stretching well beyond immediate military and economic questions. Together, for example, we must explore the possibilities of leashing the tensions of the cold war and reducing the dangers of the arms race. Together we must work to strengthen the spirit of those Europeans who are now not free, to reestablish their old ties to freedom and the West, so that their desire for liberty, and their sense of nationhood, and their sense of belonging to the Western community will survive for future expression. We ask those who would be our adversaries to understand that in our relations with them we will not bargain one nation's interests against another's and that the commitment to the cause of freedom is common to us all.

All of us in the West must be faithful to our conviction that peace in Europe can never be complete until everywhere in Europe— and that includes Germany—men can choose, in peace and freedom, how their countries shall be governed and choose, without threat to any neighbor—reunification with their countrymen.

I preach no easy liberation and I make no empty promises, but my countrymen, since our country was founded, believe strongly in the proposition that all men shall be free and all free men shall have this right of choice.

As we look steadily eastward in the hope and purpose of new freedom, we must also look—and ever more closely—to our transatlantic ties. The Atlantic community will not soon become a single overarching superstate. But practical steps toward stronger common purpose are well within our means. As we widen our common effort in defense and our threefold cooperation in economics, we shall inevitably strengthen our political ties as well. Just as your current efforts for unity in Europe will produce a stronger voice in the dialog between us, so in America our current battle for the liberty and prosperity of all citizens can only deepen the meaning of our common historic purposes. In the far future there may be a new great union for us all. But for the present, there is plenty for all to do in building new and enduring connections.

In short, the words of Thucydides are a warning, not a prediction. We have it in us, as 18 years have shown, to build our defenses, to strengthen our economies, and to tighten our political bonds, both in good weather and in bad. We can move forward with the confidence that is born of success and the skill that is born of experience. And as we move, let us take heart from the certainty that we are not only united by danger and necessity but by hope and purpose as well.

For we know now that freedom is more than the rejection of tyranny, that prosperity is more than an escape from want, that partnershp is more than a sharing of power. These are all, above all, great human adventures. They must have meaning and conviction and purpose—and because they do, in your country now and in mine, in all the nations of the alliance, we are called to a great new mission.

It is not a mission of self-defense alone, for that is a means, not an end. It is not a mission of arbitrary power—for we reject the idea that one nation should dominate another. The mission is to create a new social order, founded on liberty and justice, in which men are the masters of their fate, in which states are the servants of their citizens, and in which all men and women can share a better life for themselves and their children. That is the object of our common policy.

To realize this vision, we must seek, above all, a world of peace—a world in which peoples dwell together in mutual respect and work together in mutual regard, a world where peace is not a mere interlude between wars but an incentive to the creative energies of humanity. We will not find such a peace today, or even tomorrow. The obstacles to hope are large and menacing. Yet the goal of a peaceful world must—today and tomorrow—shape our decisions and inspire our purposes.

So we are all idealists. We are all visionaries. Let it not be said of this Atlantic generation that we left ideals and visions to the past, nor purpose and determination to our adversaries. We have come too far, we have sacrificed too much, to disdain the future now. And we shall ever remember what Goethe told us, that the "highest wisdom, the best that mankind ever knew" was the realization that "he only earns his freedom and existence who daily conquers them anew."

17

President Kennedy in Berlin, June 26, 1963

President Kennedy delivering "Ich bin ein Berliner" address, West Berlin, June 26, 1963. Left, Chancellor Adenauer; right, Governing Mayor of West Berlin Willy Brandt.

On June 26, 1963, President Kennedy addressed the people of Berlin in front of the Schoeneberg city hall:

I am proud to come to this city as a guest of your distinguished Mayor, who has symbolized throughout the world the fighting spirit of West Berlin. And I am proud to visit the Federal Republic with your distinguished Chancellor, who for some years has committed Germany to democracy and freedom and progress, and to come here in the company of my fellow American General Clay, who has been in this city during its great moments of crisis and will come again if ever needed.

Two thousand years ago, the proudest boast was "I am a Roman"—"Civis Romanus sum." Today, in the world of freedom, the proudest boast is "Ich bin ein Berliner."

"Let Them Come To Berlin—"

There are many people in the world who really don't understand—
or say they don't—what is the great issue between the free world
and the Communist world. Let them come to Berlin. There are
some who say that Communism is the wave of the future. Let them
come to Berlin. And there are some who say in Europe and elsewhere: We can work with the Communists. Let them come to Berlin. And there are even a few who say that it is true that Communism
is an evil system, but it permits us to make economic progress. Let
them come to Berlin.

"Democracy Needs No all"

Freedom has many difficulties and democracy is not perfect, but
we have never had to put a wall up to keep our people in—to prevent
them from leaving us.

I want to say, on behalf of my countrymen who live many
miles away on the other side of the Atlantic, who are far distant
from you, that they take the greatest pride that they have been
able to share with you, even from a distance, the story of the last
18 years. I know of no town, no city, that has been besieged for 18
years, that still lives with the vitality and the force and the hope
and the determination of the city of West Berlin.

"Dividing A People"

While the wall is the most obvious and vivid demonstration of the
failure of the Communist system, for all the world to see, we take
no satisfaction in it, for it is, as your Mayor has said, an offense not
only against history but an offense against humanity, separating
families, dividing husbands and wives and brothers and sisters and
dividing a people who wish to be joined together.

What is true of this city is true of Germany. Real, lasting
peace in Europe can never be assured as long as one German out
of four is denied the elementary right of free men; and that is to
make a free choice. In 18 years of peace and good faith this generation of Germans has earned a right to be free, including the right
to unite their families and their nation in lasting peace with good
will to all people.

"I Am A Berliner"

You live in a defended island of freedom, but your life is part of the
main. So let me ask you as I close to lift your eyes beyond the
dangers of today to the hopes of tomorrow—beyond the freedom
merely of this city of Berlin or your country of Germany to the

advance of freedom everywhere, beyond the Wall to the day of peace with justice, beyond yourselves and ourselves to all mankind. Freedom is indivisible, and when one man is enslaved all are not free. When all are free then we can look forward to that day when this city will be joined as one, and this country, and this great continent of Europe in a peaceful and hopeful globe. When that day finally comes, as it will, the people of West Berlin can take sober satisfaction in the fact that they were in the front lines for almost two decades.

All free men, wherever they may live, are citizens of Berlin, and therefore as a free man, I take pride in the words: "Ich bin ein Berliner."

18

Address by Chancellor Erhard in New York, June 11, 1964

Chancellor Erhard and President Johnson at the White House, Washington, during visit to U.S. June 11 – 13, 1964.

Chancellor Ludwig Erhard (who succeeded Chancellor Adenauer on Oct. 16, 1963) addressed the Council on Foreign Relations in New York while on a visit to the United States June 11 – 13, 1964:

The fact that the theme of my address can be "Germany in the Alliance of Free Nations" is due to the far-sightedness and political wisdom of great men, including some from your country.

In speaking on this theme, I am tempted to quote a phrase by Ben Gurion: "He who does not believe in miracles, is no realist." Although I cannot embrace this point of view, I understand it. I cannot embrace it because in politics the word "miracle," or "economic miracle" is not helpful. In fact TIME magazine even asserts that the beauty of German girls has brought about still another miracle that probably has nothing to do with politics.

Germany Indebted To U.S. And Its Statesmen

Some of the alleged miracles can be explained. For the political and economic development of the free part of Germany, however, there was only one realistic guide-line:

"To overcome the demons of the past, to work diligently and to help build a new future together with the free peoples of the world."

We have tried our best to build a new and better order out of the political and human tragedy that occurred in Germany. In this connection, let me mention the names of those who deserve credit for our rebirth. First, my predecessor, Konrad Adenauer, next, Heinrich von Brentano and public personalities such as Theodor Heuss and Erich Ollenhauer, among others.

But all our efforts could not have been successful without the understanding and generous help of the victorious powers, above all of the United States of America. To Presidents Harry S. Truman and Dwight D. Eisenhower, to my friends Lucius Clay and John McCloy, and last but not least to the great Briton Winston Churchill, the enduring gratitude of the whole German nation is due.

Had the Western world not generously offered its hand to defeated Germany, postwar history would probably—despite the rejection of Communism by our people—have taken a different course. The leading statesmen of the Western powers, however, were not only politically wise but also were human enough to help open the path to a new peaceful future for the German people.

Thus, they made possible the reconstruction of Germany and its inclusion into the alliance of free nations. This was one of the happiest events of providence in German history, and for the future, I hope, of all free peoples.

New Germany Based On Respect For Law

Please allow me to say a word concerning this new Germany: Viewed from the United States today, I know that Germany sometimes offers a conflicting picture. To you, this new Germany can be a country of economic prosperity and political stability, but it is also—and I am well aware of it—a country in which shameful deeds, among the most horrible to which human beings have lowered themselves, are still to be judged.

The re-integration of the Federal Republic into the community of free peoples can be regarded as achieved only when we have liberated ourselves from the last dregs now cropping up again in gruesome trials. Even when these trials are exploited by propaganda, we accept it—because nothing is more important for us than to show to the world that we put law, justice and an awareness of the law before everything. We shall bring everyone to justice who in the service of Nazism has become a criminal by murdering, torturing, robbing and blackmailing.

Germany Continues Restitution

On the other hand, in a free state based on law, mere political errors of the individual must not again lead to a witch hunt. The mere political confusion of a human being cannot and must not during his whole lifetime be a mark of Cain and make of him a pariah.

What would the world be if we did not accept as reconciliation a change of mind, genuine purification and better insight? This coming to grips of the German people with its past is closely interrelated with its reconciliation with itself, and it constitutes the will to peaceful construction of the present and the determination to work closely together with all peoples of good will.

Germany will therefore continue to make good the injustice which has been committed in its name, to make amends to the victims as far as one can atone through material compensation. We regard this restitution as a binding obligation and hope that just and fair solutions, also for those areas which are still open, can be found together with those concerned.

World Position Of Germany

Let me now describe the position of Germany in the world. That means I must speak about "European Policy," about problems of the "Atlantic Alliance" and the position of Germany in the East-West conflict.

We want the unification of Europe out of our deepest conviction, and therefore we have worked for two decades for European integration, not only because it is a sound concept from an economic point of view or because it increases our security, but most of all because, looking ahead to the decades to come, the nations of Europe will only be able to master their destiny and have a future if they unite.

In addition, the emancipation of the peoples of Asia and Africa into independent states has changed the political landscape of our planet from the ground up. Seen historically, Europe has a chance (and freedom in the long run can be safeguarded) only if the United States finds an equal partner in the union of the free nations of Europe, a partner which gives to the free part of our continent that political and economic strength which is indispensable in making us safe from every menace against our life and our common existence and which will enable us to master the great tasks of the future.

German-French Friendship Basis For Peace

For such a European policy, our friendship with France offers a firm and lasting foundation.

This is precisely where the value of the German-French Treaty lies. This reconciliation has shown to all the world that where there is a strong political will, even so-called "arch-enmities" can be overcome. Beyond this example, we believe that friendly and good-neighborly relationships create firm ground for mutual respect and an understanding of the traditions, ties and way of life of other peoples.

Even if we do not always agree with France on important political questions, we are aware, on the other hand, that without the friendship between our two countries, Europe can never be united.

What German-French reconciliation means, not only for America but far beyond, becomes evident if we recall that World War I broke out fifty years ago and World War II twenty-five years ago. That both wars caused your country heavy losses was due, not to a small degree, to the infamous enmity between France and Germany.

This danger no longer exists. The meaning and inherent pattern of this historical change, for which President de Gaulle is largely responsible, will clear the way to a politically and economically united Greater Europe which, in turn, remains the basic condition for a genuine Atlantic Community.

Europe As An Equal Partner

In the economic as well as the political sector, we Germans have always dreamed of a Europe that would be open to all free European countries. We want, I repeat, "a Europe of the Free and Equal," in which neither size nor power are the decisive factors. We want a Europe in which the nations will enjoy a new cultural birth while preserving their heritage, a Europe which combines its economic and social resources in order to live up in equal measure to its political and humanitarian tasks.

Not a divided but only a united Europe, with a clear policy and mutual political goals, is able to meet its responsibility in world politics. Atlantic partnership is possible only with Europe as an equal partner.

Even a Europe thus united, however, depends on a firm alliance with the United States with whom it feels closely related in tradition and in the striving for freedom, justice and a just order in the world. To no less degree, the United States must be concerned that Europe remains a part of the Free World and is not drawn into the power sphere of Communism. For, if free Europe should perish America would be no more than an island surrounded by Communist states.

We will continue to do our utmost in the future to strengthen the ties between Europe and the United States, especially the unity within NATO. We are willing to share further the mutual efforts and burdens, and especially to cooperate with the United States and other allies in buiding up the Multilateral Force.

Defense Of Freedom Is Interdependent

As much as certain developments within the NATO Alliance give room for concern, we must nevertheless realize that all partners to the Alliance recognize the interdependence of the defense of freedom throughout the world.

For us, this means that we must not only have an intellectual understanding for genuine problems of the United States, in Cuba or Southeast Asia for instance, but that we are ready to support actively the policy of our Atlantic ally within the reach of our possibilities. Our possibilities here lie in the political and economic fields.

Here and there today one meets with the opinion that responsibility for freedom in Southeast Asia or Berlin and the recognition of the right of self-determination for the German people should be left solely to the peoples and governments immediately concerned. However, freedom in the world is forfeited and lost unless we all stand up for it everywhere and keep alive our idea of a just order.

A lessening of the feeling of solidarity in the Western world undoubtedly represents a great danger. We would fall prey to grave illusions if we believed that the danger of Communism had decreased simply because language and tactics have changed within the other camp. Now, as ever, we have every reason to remain vigilant.

"Peaceful Coexistence" Traced From Stalin To Khrushchev

The road to a true and durable relaxation is still far off and—we should not deceive ourselves—there are many pitfalls along the way.

The Soviets today openly declare themselves in favor of the principle of "peaceful coexistence" and of commercial competition with the West. The slogan of peaceful coexistence is hardly a new one.

Back in 1927, Stalin already had made it the principle of his policy. But that did not prevent him from dividing Poland together with Hitler, from attacking Finland, from expanding his sphere of power far into the middle of Europe, from triggering the attack on Korea. Was it not Khrushchev, while adhering to coexistence, which he limited as to time, who in 1958 initiated the Berlin crisis and in 1962 the Cuba crisis? A genuine change of attitude can only be demonstrated by deeds.

For some time it has been evident that Khrushchev is ready to reach an agreement in some areas with the West. The Federal Republic welcomes any tendency towards a real détente and hopes that this display of amity is not meant only to help bridge the period in which the Soviet Union is busy with the economic and political difficulties of the Eastern bloc. Unquestionably, American firmness during the Berlin and Cuba crises did not fail to make an impression.

Germans Prepared To Contribute Toward Détente

Some aspects of Soviet policy raise hopes among us. From hope radiate strength and willpower. But hope can also be deceptive. It is, therefore, necessary to be watchful and to draw a sharp line between hope and illusion and not to lose our direction.

We should never forget that the origin of world tension was the unacceptable demands of Communism for continuous expansion of its sphere of power and the violation of people's rights.

In this connection the view is sometimes voiced that we Germans should also contribute to normalization and relaxation of tension. We are prepared to do this. But it would be irresponsible and an imposition to demand from Germany a readiness for self-sacrifice and the renunciation of the divided country's right of self-determination as a contribution to normalization.

No one in the world can expect a better and peaceful future while a great number of our people are indefinitely denied their human rights.

Mutual Concessions Needed For True Détente

The desire for peaceful solutions calls for readiness to make mutual concessions. We appreciate the Soviet interest in having reliable guaranties that the events of 1941 will not be repeated. We have said this many times.

Hitler's violation of his promises and his aggression naturally stunned the Russian people. This at least partly explains the cry for security despite Russia's overwhelming military superiority. It is for this reason that the Federal Republic time and again has emphasized its readiness for general, controlled disarmament. It has placed all its fighting troops under the command of NATO.

Back in 1954, in accordance with the principle of human rights, it renounced the use of force and the production of ABC-weapons. The Federal Republic is not seeking for itself the power of decision over the use of atomic weapons. It has suggested complete and free travel between East and West, also with respect to the exchange of publications. It is trying to intensify economic and cultural contacts despite very noticeable attempts at political blackmail.

The Soviet reaction towards our honest efforts was always a demand for concessions as a prerequisite for negotiations. Taking the initiative when it provides only for one-way performances has nothing in common with a true détente.

Soviets Still Demand Partition Of German People

At times, unofficial Western quarters suggested that we familiarize ourselves with the substance of such "détente projects." The desire to loosen up rigid fronts is indeed shared by the German Government; still, we must not yield to impatient parties just for the sake of a situation which looks dangerous. It is a matter of doing the right thing at the right time.

As you know, there have been proposals in which the Soviets were even offered a price for the surrender of what the West holds incontestably. For instance, let us take the right of unimpaired access to Berlin which the West has held since 1945. It would be a truly strange idea to obtain the confirmation of such access by the Soviet Union and, in exchange, abandon decisive political principles such as the non-recognition of the brutal despotic regime in the Soviet-occupied Zone.

The Soviet Union still demands, as before, the recognition of the police-state regime of the Soviet Zone and the partition of the German people.

What is the truth of the political situation? The entire world is a witness to the crimes of this regime. It is a tragic "reality" which more than three million refugees can report on. There would certainly be many more if it were not for the Wall and barbed wire which prevents Germans from fleeing the alleged blessings of this regime.

Thus the problem is as follows: Would peace really be secured if the present line of demarcation between us and the Soviet Zone would become a border between states? The opposite is true. We need only be reminded that the Polish people, which was prevented by its neighbors from uniting for more than a century, never gave up its desire for national unity and finally realized it in the end.

The German people also will never reconcile itself with partition. We are convinced that moderation serves to maintain peace. We have indeed always defended our right to live, but nevertheless we have exercised restraint.

Germany's Neighbors To The East

Let me say also a few words about our relationship to our neighbors in the East. For centuries, these relations have been close and—contrary to prevailing opinion—fruitful and largely friendly. Our history is tied up with theirs in many common areas. Historically viewed, periods of crisis and enmities are hardly more significant than episodes, in spite of their coming to a head after World War I.

The greatest strain, almost disastrous, in the relationship between the German people and the East European nations was Hitler's brutal policy of force. Today, we are still suffering the consequences of this destructive policy. Therefore, we will do everything in our power to overcome this tragic situation.

Today, Communist governments rule in the East European countries. Nevertheless, these countries belong to Europe. We see our job as building bridges, healing the sufferings of Europe as far as it is possible for us to do, and—beyond the realm of ideologies—fostering contacts with all thinking, open-minded people not addicted to dogma in those countries.

Last year, we exchanged trade representations with most of these countries, and we are making efforts to improve these economic relations. We hope that we will also be able to intensify cultural exchange and to encourage the understanding of mutual problems.

Germany Has No Claims To Czech Territory

Today, the only direct neighbor of the Federal Republic among the East European countries is Czechoslovakia. Unfortunately, the policy of the Federal Republic of Germany toward Czechoslovakia has recently not been clear.

I, therefore, state here explicitly and clearly: The Munich Agreement of 1938 was torn to pieces by Hitler. The German Government has no territorial claims whatsoever with regard to Czechoslovakia and separates itself expressly from any declarations which have given rise to a different interpretation.

On the Oder-Neisse Line: In 1945, Stalin in cold calculation advanced Polish territory deeply into Germany in order to estrange the German and the Polish peoples as enemies forever. About 10 million Germans were expelled from their homes.

The German Government feels that the German-Polish border should be established in a peace treaty in accordance with the Potsdam Agreement, a treaty that can only be concluded with an all-German government. Poland and the Federal Republic of Germany have a common interest that this condition be established, which will make it possible for the two peoples to live together in peace.

Just Order In Europe Is German Goal

Communist propaganda presents daily to the world the phantom of a revengeful Germany. The fact is, however, that we do not pursue a policy of revenge nor of restoration, neither today nor in the future.

We have shown, through close cooperation with our Western neighbors in the new order of Europe, that we are setting our sights beyond the limits of pre-war Europe. The political, economic and technical development is advancing further to establish new ways of life.

The goal of our policy toward the West as well as toward the East is to establish a just new European order, based on peaceful agreements, where people of all nations can live together as free and good neighbors, and where the importance of borders will fade into the background.

Let us not forget: In the Berlin issue, Moscow has repeatedly made attempts to break up the Western front. The question of granting passes to and from East Berlin is a good point to show that the Soviet Union assesses the damage done by its short-sighted policy of force and factional interests.

The Wall does not fit into the image of "humanitarian Communism." Military preponderance alone is no longer an argument which convinces. Berlin is obvious testimony for everyone of the superiority of freedom over coercion. The allies are in Berlin on the basis of a legal status of their own which does not depend on approval by the Soviets.

The fact that the Russians have a high respect for Allied rights or at least for their effect on third parties is revealed by their constant attempts to obtain a change. Berlin embodies not only the hope of people living in the Soviet Zone but a good part of the will to live of all free nations.

Germany Desires Easing Of Tensions

Our "no" to Communist demands has nothing to do with either a nationalist outlook or a lack of imagination. It is simply the knowledge that no people can be denied the fulfillment of its political task without destroying its vitality.

Our allies have voiced their interest in a greater German share in the common defense and also in greater German participation regarding aid for the young nations. In this connection, however, it should also be borne in mind that a Germany weakened to please Moscow would not be capable of carrying greater burdens within the framework of the Atlantic Community.

It would amount to squaring the circle to want to create a Germany which is unimportant enough to calm Soviet anxieties in Europe, but strong enough to be able to confront with greater effort the Communist offensive all over the world. We must all make sure that every step we take helps the common cause.

To eliminate any misinterpretations, let me state the following: We do not want less but rather more easing of tensions. For instance, we would like to see the Soviets extend the principle of "peaceful coexistence" by agreeing also to a coexistence of ideas.

Germans Seek Improved Relations With Soviets

Above all, we wish and expect that the efforts to ease tensions are directed from political peripheral areas to certain political issues. These major issues, which can give rise to the development of international crises, must not be eliminated from the East-West talks. Their solution will show whether the will of the Soviets to ease tensions is genuine or merely a tactical maneuver.

We know, however, that an effective détente does not depend on the great powers alone. Their responsibility regarding the German question is inescapable. But that means that the Federal Government, as well, must strive to the best of its ability for an improvement in German-Soviet relations.

The government, as well as the whole German people, is free of "cold war" ideas; they are ready for any meaningful discussion. But no one thinks that the Germans should go it alone. There will not be a new Rapallo nor will there be a new Munich.

Reunification Is In Best Interest Of All

Settlement of the German question through self-determination is by no means outside of but an integral part of the policy of détente, our strategy for peace. It is the very key which opens the doors to a better and peaceful future.

Indeed, in the final analysis, this also applies to the Soviet Union. Reunification through self-determination is in the best interest of the people; it is in the best interest of all East European peoples. At any rate, it offers better guarantees of security and prosperity than the current kind of imperialism based on terror and suppression still practiced in the Soviet Zone of Germany.

We hope, and there are beginning to be slight indications to justify this hope, that this conviction is gaining ground even in the Soviet Union.

May I assure you, my American friends, that a free and united German people will be a source of peace and security for Europe. We realize that the freedom you helped us recover imposes upon us the primary obligation to defend that freedom against all enemies within and without, and to live in peace with our neighbors.

I know—and I now refer to what I said in my opening remarks—that it was a courageous decision on the part of the Western statesmen to grant us aid and freedom. But it should also be said, and this is to our credit, that they need not regret that decision for it helped clarify all disputes between our Western neighbors and us and to overcome prejudices that had been passed on from one generation to another.

It helped establish a firm and friendly relationship between ourselves and our former enemies and made possible a continuing economic and political cooperation in Europe that only a short time ago seemed inconceivable.

Germans Seek Progress For All Mankind

When the Germans in the Soviet-occupied zone are finally granted the right of self-determination, when the German people are again able to live under one freely-elected government, then it will be possible to establish a close and peaceful cooperation between ourselves and the East European states. One of the most dangerous trouble spots would thus be eliminated and a basis created for normalizing the situation in Middle Europe and reaching a true détente.

There is no longer an outlook that could be called purely American, or purely Anglo-Saxon, purely German or purely French, indeed, not even purely European. Here and there the remnants of ideas about power politics which brought the Western world close to destruction may still be effective. But such misconceived nationalism is a thing of the past.

True love of one's country can thrive only under a world-embracing idea of the kind Johann Gottfried Herder meant when he said that dedication to the cause of one's people is justified only "if a step forward for the benefit of a people is at the same time a step forward for the whole of mankind."

This is the path along which the German people want to go with you.

19

Dinner Speech by Chancellor Erhard on the Occasion of His Meeting With President Johnson, September 26, 1966

Chancellor Erhard visited Washington September 24–28, 1966, for discussions with the U.S. Administration. In a dinner speech on September 26, the Chancellor stressed the common values and interests which would overcome any temporary differences of opinion:

Mr. President, Mrs. Johnson:

I would like, Mr. President, to thank you from the bottom of my heart for the warm welcome that you have extended to me and, very particularly, to Mrs. Erhard, to my colleagues, and to the members of my delegation.

I have felt, today, how closely and how long we belong to each other. If I say long, I am thinking in terms of my activities in German political life which reach back to the time of the breakdown.

I am thinking about, too, the happy experiences which became alive again today when I met so many people with whom, from the very beginning, I cooperated in rebuilding our country.

I won't be able to name them all, but I would like to name a few of them on behalf of all. General Lucius Clay, Mr. McCloy, General Taylor—as I say, I can't name them all.

But I have again felt something of the good will and open mindedness with which the American people met us in the darkest hour of our nation. And that, Mr. President, will remain unforgotten.

This is a lasting bond and this, in fact, has brought about the community of ideals which we share in common. In the beginning we thought that we were about to be reeducated. But soon we felt that there was much more behind it, that there was the honest will of a friend who was extending his saving hand to those who were in bitter need.

In the meantime, we have experienced, as you have said, Mr. President, that freedom needs to be conquered daily anew. And to use your words, these ideals require of us courage and firmness.

When I think of your worries which occupy you in the first line, then I can say, Mr. President, that I believe that of all of the peoples of the world there is none that has as much understanding and feels as much sympathy for the pain and at the same time the hope which the American people experience when standing up for the freedom you fight for, a just peace, and for the restoration of law and order, and that we share your hope that you be successful in restoring calm and order in that part of the world.

We do what we can do to help you in the humanitarian field. You can also be sure that the German people as a whole feel and know that there is a moral relationship between the worries you are occupied with and that move you, and worries that move the German people. I have only to quote in that context the name of Berlin.

And we cannot be sure of our freedom without making efforts daily to preserve that freedom. And in Germany there are problems still, the solution of which requires your assistance. And let me say that in trying to solve these problems we trust in you.

We have to solve the European problems, but we consider these problems imbricated into an Atlantic world and we know that what is about to form in Europe is indissolubly linked with what the Atlantic Alliance stands for with our joint effort to stand up in defense of the ideals of freedom, peace, and security.

And for us the United States of America is the country in which we place the greatest trust, with whom we feel the most intimate solidarity. We are aware that freedom, peace, security, are not words which should only be used when there is no problem and no tension, should be used only because you are sure to get applause when you use them, that they must not become the small change, that they must not become slogans. But that they must be comprehended in their total value, in what they mean as commitment for man, for peoples, for nations.

And if during these days, Mr. President, we struggle in the joint search for fruitful solutions, we know that friendship does not only have to prove its value when there is sunshine everywhere and when there is not the slightest difference in interests—we feel that these ideals must stand their test even when both our countries have, each of them, their worries. And that we must try not only to understand ours but that we must at the same time show the greatest understanding for the partner, the ally, the friend.

And I think that this was underlying all our talks. It was also underlying our internal discussions on our side, that we were trying on our side to have the maximum understanding for the American position.

And we are equally sure, Mr. President, that the same was true for the American side—that you, too, were appreciating, trying to understand, our reasons.

We don't have to use big words and I don't think there is any reason for us to give up. The problems of our world can be solved. They can be solved all the more easily, the closer we stand together. What we defend cannot be had for nothing. And we are prepared to pay the price that goes with it.

When I say "price" I don't mean that in the material sense. I mean it in terms of the willingness of peoples to assume the sacrifices that must be assumed in order to settle problems.

I was very pleased, Mr. President, that you have opened this hope and I do believe that it is and I do hope that it is more than only hope: the expectation that soon we shall be able to welcome you in Germany. And then, of course, Mr. President, we expect to welcome you and Mrs. Johnson. And I am sure that the reception you will have in Germany, not only from the Government, but from the people, will be a welcome with open arms. Because the German people understand that you are a symbol of this world and that we share a common fate.

Some people may think that this is a historical accident. I think it is important. I think that there is a common spirit animating us and this common spirit must not be lost, because otherwise cruelty and force would prevail in the world.

We must be vigilant. We must be strong. But we must also trust in the moral force which will guarantee freedom, peace, and the order of law.

I would like to toast looking forward to having our next meeting, Mr. President, take place in Germany, and then you will find that this is visible confirmation of the friendship between our two nations, a friendship which is lasting.

20

Joint Statement Following Discussions Between President Johnson and Chancellor Erhard, September 27, 1966

The text of the joint statement of Sept. 27, 1966, reads as follows:

President Johnson and Chancellor Erhard completed today the fifth of a series of meetings which began in 1963. The two leaders attach exceptional importance to these consultations, which afford an opportunity for intimate and thorough discussion of matters of mutual concern. They were accompanied by Secretary of State Rusk, Secretary of the Treasury Fowler and Secretary of Defense McNamara on the American side and Federal Ministers Dr. Schroeder, von Hassel and Dr. Westrick on the German side.

In two days of wide-ranging talks the President and the Chancellor reviewed problems in the relations between the two countries, as well as questions of world peace and security. The exchange of views, as in former meetings, took place in an open and cordial atmosphere and resulted in basic agreement on all important points. The President and the Chancellor found that the Federal Republic of Germany and the United States of America continue to share a deep community of interest in all major problems affecting international security.

The situation of the Atlantic Alliance and the state of East-West relations, including the problem of a divided Germany and Berlin, were among the main topics discussed. Questions of long-term Atlantic defense planning, which include the burden on the American balance of payments resulting from the stationing of United States forces in Europe were also discussed in that context. Other subjects reviewed were disarmament and the non-proliferation of nuclear weapons, European unity within an Atlantic partnership, the Vietnam conflict, foreign aid, space and other scientific cooperation, the Kennedy Round and international liquidity.

German Reunification

President Johnson reaffirmed the objective of the reunification of Germany as one of the most significant goals of American foreign policy. Chancellor Erhard stressed the human suffering which results from the continuing artificial division of Germany, and the President and the Chancellor agreed that a solution of the German problem on the basis of self-determination was essential in the interest of humanity as well as of lasting peace in Europe. They emphasized the right and duty of the Government of the Federal Republic of Germany, as the only freely elected Government of the German people, to speak and to stand for their interests until the German nation has been made whole. They agreed that the freedom of Berlin must be preserved and that the problem of Berlin can be resolved only within the framework of the peaceful reunification of Germany.

Western Unity And East-West Relations

The President and the Chancellor addressed two main needs of our day: Western unity and improved East-West relations.

The President and the Chancellor underlined once more the great importance of European unification founded on common action and common institutions. A united Europe is a basic element of Western strength and freedom and a bulwark against the spirit of national rivalry which has produced so many disasters in the past. They emphasized that Europe and North America are parts of a common Atlantic world and have a common fate. It therefore continues to be a vital interest of their foreign policies to multiply and deepen the ties between North America and a uniting Europe. In this connection the President and the Chancellor discussed the problem of the technological gap between the United States and Europe and noted the excellent initiatives of the Italian Government in this regard. The President indicated that the United States stands ready to respond to any proposals by our European allies in this area of advanced technology.

In East-West relations they believe that we should continue to respond to the widespread yearning to heal the division of Europe and of Germany without which no lasting peace can be achieved, looking steadily for ways to overcome the rigidities of the past.

They believe that closer ties between all European nations, the United States and the Soviet Union will serve this purpose. So will new moves to remove ancient fears.

They agreed to explore with their allies every useful step that could be taken to these ends.

The Chancellor discussed with the President the possibilities for further development of the ideas expressed in the German Peace Note of March 25, 1966. The President welcomed this constructive German initiative.

The President and the Chancellor are convinced that Western unity will contribute to East-West understanding—that Western European integration and Atlantic solidarity can open the way for wider cooperation in promoting the security and well-being of Europe as a whole.

Atlantic Security

President Johnson and Chancellor Erhard discussed fully the problems of Atlantic security. They agreed that tension in Europe is less acute. Yet a basic threat to security persists and the Atlantic Alliance continues to be the vital condition of peace and freedom. They reaffirmed the determination of the two governments to maintain the strength of the Alliance and its integrated defense and to adjust it to the requirements it will face in the coming years. They agreed that a searching reappraisal should be undertaken of the threat to security and, taking into account changes in military technology and mobility, of the forces required to maintain adequate deterrence and defense. This review should also address the question of equitable sharing of the defense and other comparable burdens, and the impact of troop deployment and force levels on the balance of payments of the United States and United Kingdom, and take into account the effect on the German economic and budgetary situation of measures designed to ameliorate balance of payments problems.

The President and Chancellor agreed that it would be desirable to have conversations in which the United Kingdom would be invited to participate along with the Federal Republic and the United States, to examine these questions, in the consideration of which all the NATO allies will wish to participate.

The President and Chancellor worked on the problems which have arisen under the existing offset arrangements between the Federal Republic and the United States. The Chancellor assured the President that the Federal Republic would make every effort fully to meet the current offset agreement insofar as financial arrangements affecting the balance of payments are involved. The Chancellor explained to the President that the Federal Republic would not in the future be able fully to offset the foreign exchange costs associated with the stationing of U.S. forces in Germany by the purchasing of military equipment. It was agreed that that question would be one of the problems to be considered in the tripartite conversations.

NATO Nuclear Issues

The President and the Chancellor emphasized their great interest in an early termination of the armaments race and in progress in the field of general and controlled disarmament.

They agreed that the proliferation of nuclear weapons into the national control of non-nuclear states must be checked, and expressed the view that nuclear arrangements consistent with this objective should be made within the Alliance to provide the non-nuclear Allies with an appropriate share in nuclear defense. They noted with satisfaction the decision of the Nuclear Planning Working Group in Rome to recommend a permanent nuclear planning committee in the Alliance. They hope other members of the Alliance will support this recommendation, which would broaden and deepen the areas of nuclear consultation and would bring the Allies more intimately into planning for nuclear defense.

Vietnam

President Johnson informed Chancellor Erhard of the current situation in Vietnam. Chancellor Erhard reiterated his view that the assistance given by the United States to Vietnam's resistance against aggression is important to the entire free world. Chancellor Erhard stated that in his view the efforts and sacrifices made by the United States in Vietnam provide assurance of the seriousness with which the United States regards its international commitments. The Chancellor expressed his deep regret that the President's repeated peace offers have so far not been accepted. President Johnson expressed to Chancellor Erhard great appreciation for this support and for the tangible assistance in the economic and humanitarian fields which the Federal Republic has given to Vietnam.

Space And Science Cooperation

The President and the Chancellor discussed possibilities for increased cooperation in technology and science and in particular in the field of space research. The Chancellor expressed his satisfaction that effective steps towards increased cooperation in space research have been initiated since his last meeting with the President in December 1965. The President and the Chancellor welcomed the decision to expand the present cooperative satellite program reached as a result of the recent discussions in Bonn between NASA Administrator Webb and Minister of Science Stoltenberg.

The President and the Chancellor agreed that scientific cooperation should be pressed forward for the mutual benefit of both countries and the advancement of human knowledge, preserving opportunities for additional nations to participate and contribute.

Natural Resources And Environmental Control Cooperation

The President and the Chancellor expressed great satisfaction over progress which has been made on the program of German-American cooperation in the field of natural resources and environmental control which was agreed on during the Chancellor's visit last December. They reviewed with satisfaction the visit of Secretary of the Interior Udall to Germany in March of this year with a mission to look into what we could learn from each other. American and German program directors and expert teams have been appointed who are exchanging experiences and making detailed plans, especially in the fields of air and water pollution and urban renewal.

Kennedy Round

The President and the Chancellor discussed the Kennedy Round. They agreed that the European Communities and the United States are now facing the decisive and most difficult phase of these trade negotiations. Both governments will give a very high priority to their successful conclusion in order to achieve the common goal of encouraging increased world trade by a substantial reduction in trade barriers.

International Monetary Negotiations

The President and the Chancellor also discussed the international monetary negotiations. They expressed satisfaction with the decisions of the Ministers and the Governors of the Group of 10 at the Hague, and with the plan for joint meetings between the International Monetary Fund Executive Directors and the deputies of the Group of 10. They agreed that the successful conclusion of these negotiations is of the highest political importance.

The President proposed to the Chancellor that there be established secure means of direct telephonic communication between Washington and Bonn to permit easy and rapid consultation on issues of concern to the two Governments. The Chancellor agreed that such an arrangement would be useful and should be set up as soon as feasible.

The two leaders agreed to increase the flow between their countries of the young people who are devoted to excellence in special fields. A competitive scholarship program will be explored to provide a creative exchange of talented youth who can make serious scientific, cultural or artistic contributions to the society of the host country.

The President and the Chancellor were happy to have had this opportunity to discuss together their common problems, as well as to renew their close personal friendship. They reaffirmed the friendship and trust which has developed between the people and governments of the United States and Germany. They expressed gratification at the results achieved by this meeting which should go far toward building even closer relations between themselves and with their partners, as well as toward improving future relations with the Eastern neighbors and other parts of the world.

The Chancellor extended an invitation to the President to visit the Federal Republic next spring; the President said that he would be most pleased to do so if his responsibilities permitted.

21

Remarks by President Johnson and Chancellor Kiesinger at Welcoming Ceremonies in Washington, August 15, 1967

President Johnson receiving Chancellor Kiesinger at the White House, Washington, August 15, 1967. At right, rear: Secretary of State Rusk and Foreign Minister Brandt.

Chancellor Kurt Georg Kiesinger (who succeeded Chancellor Erhard on December 1, 1966) called on President Johnson for the first time during a visit to the United States August 14–17, 1967. In remarks at the welcoming ceremonies, both leaders placed the planned discussions within the larger context of German-American relations:

The President. Mr. Chancellor, Mrs. Kiesinger,
Mr. Vice Chancellor, distinguished guests,
ladies and gentlemen:

Mrs. Johnson and I are delighted, Mr. Chancellor, to welcome you and Mrs. Kiesinger and your distinguished associates who have come with you to the United States. We greet you with the honors and respect due the leader of a great free nation—and with the very warm affection that we feel for close and trusted friends.

The relationship between our peoples has a long history. Our German ancestors helped to build this country of ours. They contributed much of this country's greatness. German poets and scholars, philosophers and artists, scientists and churchmen—whose work is the common property of all mankind—have truly enriched the national life of America.

In the past two decades, we have worked shoulder to shoulder to build together a prosperous and a free Europe, and a prosperous and a free Germany. And, Mr. Chancellor, together we have been remarkably successful.

Mr. Chancellor, I recall with pleasure our first meeting at Bonn earlier this year. Then, as on earlier visits to your country, I saw a great democratic nation risen from the ruins of war. I saw a free people living in prosperity and dedicated to the cause of freedom. I saw a nation pledged to protect that freedom and pledged to protect that prosperity—and those of her allies as well—through the alliance which for almost two decades has sheltered us all.

Our meetings here in the White House today and tomorrow will continue our earlier friendly conversations in Bonn. They will give us an opportunity to discuss the important—yes—the numerous problems facing our two countries, facing the alliance, and facing the world.

Yesterday's triumphs can give us heart—and direction—for today's challenges. We have stood together to secure the safety of Europe. Today we stand ready to assure its future. We here in America are ready, as well, to work with you in the great task of ending the artificial division of your country.

Though Europe remains fixed in our attentions, both of us, I know, must be aware of the very urgent responsibilities that face us in other parts of the world.

In Southeast Asia, aggression by terror and warfare tests the proposition that nations have the right to chart their own paths in peace.

Tensions now strain the stability of the Middle East.

And the oldest enemies that mankind knows—poverty, hunger, disease, and ignorance—continue to master vast areas of the world in which we live.

These are problems that constantly press all of us for attention, even beyond the borders of our alliance. They can be ignored only at the peril of our own security. For distance cannot confine them. They threaten to erode the structure of peace throughout the world.

Mr. Chancellor, I look forward with great pleasure to exchanging views and ideas with you. I hope that our talks together will reinforce the already great confidence and cooperation that exists between the American people and the German people.

We are so glad that you are here. We hope that you will enjoy your stay.

The Chancellor. Mr. President, Mrs. Johnson,
ladies and gentlemen:

Mrs. Kiesinger and I, Vice Chancellor Brandt, and my associates are most cordially grateful to you, Mr. President, for the solemn and warm reception you have been extending to us in this historic place, the official residence of the President of the United States of America.

I come here as the head of government of a country, a friend and ally of the United States of America. Our talks will certainly deal with problems of interest to our two countries, but they will certainly also touch upon those great questions of peace, security, and justice in the world.

In this way—you have pointed that out already—Mr. President, we are going to continue the talks we had in Bonn earlier this year, when you came over—and I may say that the German people were very grateful to you, Mr. President, for this gesture—to participate in the funeral of Konrad Adenauer.

In Bonn, we were agreed that the North Atlantic alliance, as an instrument of peace, must preserve and will preserve and strengthen peace.

You may be convinced, Mr. President, that the Federal Republic of Germany will, to the best of its capacity and ability, make its contribution. We know, and we have always been clear in our minds, that this alliance is not of an aggressive character, but it serves to safeguard peace.

We regret that conditions existing in the world today make it necessary to maintain huge armies, to maintain strong armaments. But these conditions should not keep us from, on the contrary, they should encourage us to pursue together a policy of détente in order to settle conflicts, in order to eliminate causes of conflicts, in order to overcome differences between countries, in order to create a climate of trust and confidence whch will guarantee lasting peace.

As regards these great objectives, I may say, Mr. President, that I feel in full agreement with yourself.

As regards the Federal Republic of Germany, it will certainly do whatever it can do within its field of activity and responsibility.

In Western Europe we have pursued a policy of reconciliation and cooperation with France, with whom for centuries we have been fighting and warring. We are striving for unity of all European countries, to the establishment of a Europe which will then be a friend and partner of the United States of America, and which wants to be such a friend and partner of the United States.

As regards Eastern Europe, I have, in my government declaration, extended the hand of reconciliation to these countries as well and we have already made efforts and have begun to pave the way of understanding.

We have established diplomatic relations with Romania, which the Foreign Minister recently visited. We have concluded the trade agreement with Czechoslovakia and we are also striving for friendly and neighborly relations also with Poland and the Soviet Union.

Of course, there is one great problem, one obstacle, still in the way of these efforts and that is the question of the division of our country.

Mr. President, I should like to thank you for the understanding you have been showing for this our problem and for the readiness to help us to find a just solution to this problem. We will never surrender our efforts to attain this objective, but we are also aware, in doing that, in trying to bring about the reunification of Germany, of the responsibility for peace we have also in the world.

This may be a long and thorny way, but we will never yield in our efforts.

Mr. President, I did not come over here to speak to you only of our problems. We are fully aware of the enormous problems, the enormous worries and concerns with which the United States of America is confronted and we fully see the heavy burden you have to carry on your shoulders, Mr. President.

But you may be convinced, Mr. President, that what we will be able to do, we will certainly contribute in order, at least a little bit, to mitigate or to take off some of the burden you have to carry — fully aware of the responsibility we have.

Earlier this year, we celebrated in Bonn the 20th anniversary of the initiation of the Marshall plan in the presence of distinguished guests from the United States of America. The German people know that they owe a great debt of gratitude to the United States of America for the assistance and support they have been receiving at that time and later.

And the German people want to repay at least part of that debt of gratitude by helping to support those young countries in the world which are not yet able to develop themselves to get over their situation of misery, poverty, and distress. We want to pursue that policy, together with the United States of America.

Let me conclude, Mr. President, by saying that we want to strengthen the friendship and to make this friendship with the United States of America closer, bearing in mind the words of your countryman, Emerson: "The only way to have a friend is to be one."

Thank you.

22

President Nixon's Address to the German Parliament, February 26, 1969

President Nixon addressing the Bundestag, Bonn, February 26, 1969.

President Richard Nixon visited Bonn and Berlin soon after his inauguration. On Feb. 26, 1969, President Nixon addressed the German Bundestag:

Mr. President, Mr. Chancellor, Your Excellencies,
members of the Parliament:

It is a very great honor for me to appear before this legislative body and to respond to the very generous words of welcome that I have just heard from the presiding officer of this body.

At the outset I regret that I find it necessary to have a translator. I do say, though, that having heard his translation, he had every word right—every word.

Mr. President, you spoke of some of the great items that bind our two nations and our two peoples together. I spoke at the airport this morning of the fact that we in the United States owe so much to our German heritage.

And I can speak personally on that point because the grandmother of my two daughters on their mother's side was born in Germany.

I would like to speak of those principles and ideals that will continue to bind us together in the years ahead. First the great Alliance of which we are a part. This Alliance is strong today and must be maintained in strength in the years ahead.

The success of this Alliance is indicated by the fact that in the 20 years that it has existed, that we have had peace, as far as this part of the world is concerned, and that every one of the nations in the Alliance that was free 20 years ago is free today, including the free city of Berlin.

We are bound together, too, by the economic factors that two great and productive peoples have produced in our two countries. And we know that a strong and productive German economy is essential for a strong free world economy, just as is a strong economy in the United States.

We are bound together, too, by a common dedication to the cause of peace—peace not only for ourselves but for all mankind.

As we enter what I have described as a period of negotiations with those who have been our opponents, we recognize that for those negotiations to succeed it is essential that we maintain the strength that made negotiations possible.

But having spoken of the bonds of national heritage and background, the alliance of the economic factors, those bonds that bring us together, I would add, finally, one that is demonstrated by my presence in this chamber today. We believe, both of our countries and our peoples, in representative government, in free and vigorous debate, and in free and vigorous elections.

And having just been through the ordeal of an election campaign, I wish all of you well in your campaigns. That, as I am sure you will understand, is the international language of politics, being on both sides of the same issue.

Finally, as I stand before this parliamentary body, I realize that we share so many common traditions and it is to me a very moving experience to report to you that since becoming President of the United States I have not yet had the opportunity to appear before our own Congress, and I have not yet appeared before a legislative body in any other country.

In other words, as I stand here today before this Parliament, this is the first time that I, as President of the United States, have appeared before any legislative body in the whole world.

Mr. President, I will have many honors during the period that I will hold office, but I can assure you that as one who began his political career as a Congressman and served in that post for 4 years, and who then served in our Senate for 2 years, and then served as Vice President of the United States and President of the Senate in the chair where you sit for 8 years, that there will be no honor greater than the one I have today to address my fellow legislators.

23

Welcoming Ceremony for Chancellor Brandt,
April 10, 1970

Chancellor Brandt and President Nixon on the Chancellor's arrival in Washington April 10, 1970.

On April 10, 1970, the first official meeting took place between President Nixon and Chancellor Willy Brandt, who had been elected the new head of government on Oct. 21, 1969. The exchange of remarks by President Nixon and Chancellor Brandt at the welcoming ceremony on the South Lawn on April 10, 1970, was as follows:

The President.

Mr. Chancellor, we are honored to welcome you and the members of your party to this house and to this Nation's Capital on this magnificent spring day.

Just 17 years ago this week, when I was Vice President of the United States, I welcomed another Chancellor of your country to the United States, Chancellor Adenauer—he was of a different party. And now I welcome you today.

But while your parties were different, there are certain great principles that you both stand for, and that we stand for, that are bigger than party.

We have heard your national anthem just a few minutes ago. The title of that anthem has in it the words, "unity, justice, freedom," and those principles transcend party differences and national differences. They belong to men and women who love freedom all over the world.

Mr. Chancellor, you have been to our country many times, but most Americans welcome you and remember you as I do because you were the Mayor of Berlin—and we think of Berlin, that great and free city.

And as we welcome you today, I hope that the talks that we have, and I am confident this will be the case, will contribute to the kind of freedom without which peace is meaningless and to that kind of peace which we need if we are to enjoy freedom.

We believe deeply in these values, and we are honored to receive you so that we can work together, your people and our people, toward achieving those great common goals.

The Chancellor.

Mr. President, thank you very much for your cordial words of welcome. This is a moving moment. I have often come to the United States in past years—as a member of the German Bundestag, as Governing Mayor of Berlin, as Foreign Minister. This time I am coming as Chancellor.

To us in Germany a trip of the Chancellor to Washington is more than an ordinary official visit. It gives evidence of one of the important realities of the international situation—the close partnership between the United States and the Federal Republic of Germany. At the same time it is an expression of the close cooperation between America and Europe. Both are factors of stability in a world in which there are still so many unresolved problems and so much insecurity.

Last year we celebrated here the 20th anniversary of NATO. In the Atlantic Defense Alliance we stand together because our security requirements demand it. At the same time the Alliance is the solid basis on which we try to reduce tensions and to achieve an enduring structure of peace. This is the aim of my Government's policy—and I know that it is the aim of your policy, Mr. President.

What I have just been saying indicates the essential subjects of our talks to which I am looking forward:

I think we must maintain the efficiency of the Atlantic Alliance as an instrument for safeguarding peace.

We must give positive substance to the relations between the enlarging European Community and the United States.

We must bring into good harmony our efforts, which are serious but without illusion, to improve East-West relations.

It is no exaggeration, I feel, when I say that hardly any bilateral issues exist between our two countries. We should make sure that this remains so. The people of the Federal Republic of Germany endorse and want this partnership. I take this wish to be a mandate.

This is also true of the population of West Berlin. There is no other place where the ties between the United States and Germany are so manifest. This too must remain so.

I bring to you, Mr. President, and to the American people the greetings and good will of those for whom I speak. Our cooperation is embedded in the experience of a bitter past. It is directed to the many new challenges with which the seventies confront us.

Thank you very much, Mr. President.

24

Remarks by Chancellor Brandt April 10, 1970, at a Dinner Given by President Nixon

Chancellor Brandt responded as follows to remarks by President Nixon at a White House dinner:

Mr. President, Mrs. Nixon, ladies and gentlemen:

On behalf of the German delegation and, of course, also on behalf of Mrs. Brandt and myself, I would like to thank you, Mr. President, very cordially for your impressive words. This gratitude goes also for the friendliness with which you received us and the kindness you have shown to me by inviting me to spend a few restful days at beautiful Camp David.

My words of grateful response, Mr. President, are not only meant for the present occasion. They also include appreciation of the fact that you have always favored close relations between the United States and Europe; that in doing so you have always shown understanding for the affairs of the Federal Republic of Germany, and that last, not least, the vital interests of West Berlin have been and are close to your heart.

When I mention Berlin, let me add without hesitation that the cradle of German-American friendship stood there after World War II. I think we met first in 1954, Mr. President, when I was a member of the Bundestag visiting this great country. When we met again, also that was 12 years ago, February of 1958, you as Vice President, I as Governing Mayor, you presented me with a gavel carved from the old White House wood. With that gavel I have for many years conducted meetings which dealt, in Berlin, with the inspiring work of reconstruction, but also meetings at which grim decisions had to be taken which derived from the ever-deepening division of the city, my city.

Mr. President, your visit to Bonn and West Berlin lives in our memories. Right at the beginning of your term of office you were given proof of the strength of the confidence which my fellow-countrymen place in you and in the United States. This confidence is part of the capital you cannot weigh or measure which nations invest in history. It bears interest—and it is in the duty of political leaders not to spend such interest frivolously, but to add it as an increment to the capital.

I have come to Washington at a time when it is natural to look back and necessary to look ahead. Twenty-five years have passed since the end of World War II. The ruins have gone. Hopelessness and despondency have disappeared long ago. This is—and we shall not forget it—largely a result of the American people's willingness to help and of political foresight which are so characteristic of this great country.

I say that, Mr. President, in full awareness of our debt to the men who have paved the way for us, and I am grateful that a number of these men, the fathers of the new relationship between our countries, are together with us here tonight, and whose counsel we must still heed today.

But now it is incumbent upon us to seek an ever clearer definition of our concept for the 1970's and to assist, if possible, the young generation in finding an outlook on life in conformity with their aspirations and carrying conviction.

Both in the United States and in Europe there is now—25 years after the end of the war—a new generation, and it is a restless one. Although it grew up in relative peace it is highly sensitive to the upheavals of our time. It is searching for convincing answers that hold the promise of the future. We are called upon to meet this challenge, and I believe we can meet it.

If we take the emerging new generations seriously, it would be a disservice to them if we only told them what they want to hear. I think we must tell them that there is no alternative to the long march to achieve reforms and the equally long march to secure peace.

I have said, Mr. President, it is necessary to form an idea of the future, not as wishful thinking but in terms of a world where existing division does not necessarily imply hostile confrontation but could be accepted as a point of departure for the search for patterns of cooperation.

It is certainly no accident that your formula, Mr. President, has met with such response and that there are clear indications in various places of the readiness to set out along that path. If we did not perceive such readiness also outside the Western sphere or thought it at least possible, then some of our efforts would indeed be meaningless.

This is the concept on which my Government's policy is based. We in Germany know that the painful partition of our country can only be cured if the split dividing Europe is healed. We are striving for a structure of peace in Europe under which the countries on either side of the line which today divides our continent—

as well as the world powers—will be able to achieve a higher degree of security through a higher degree of cooperation.

In our efforts we must start out from the existing situation, that is to say from realities, in order to arrive at a more normal relationship with our Eastern neighbors. We pursue this task free from illusion but with perseverance.

There have been voices that accused the Germans of being willing to plunge into a course of "Realpolitik" in a questionable sense. They implied that we tried to follow a policy of self-interest in disregard of the moral values which, of course, must also guide international policy.

I am certainly not thinking in terms of that kind of "Realpolitik" when I speak of the necessity to accept realities. Freedom, democracy, and self-determination are values which we would never renounce. Not only has their significance been borne out by our experience, they also define our moral position in world politics. Because we believe in them we made the Atlantic Alliance a cornerstone of our policy and consider the cultivation of German-American relations an overriding interest of ours.

Mr. President, I have studied with close attention your Report on a New Strategy for Peace which you submitted to Congress on February 18. It contains the statement that the United States can no more disengage from Europe than from Alaska. Let me make it quite clear: This statement works the other way around as well. Today in the second half of the 20th century, Europe can no more disengage herself from the United States than from herself.

This awareness must inevitably determine our future action and it will again and again make it essential for us to seek common answers to solve the problems—they will sometimes certainly not be easy ones—which are related to the continued and adequate military presence of the United States in Europe without which there can be no security for all of us; to solve the problems with regard to the economic relations between America and Europe which arise from the development and the envisaged enlargement of the Common Market, and to ensure continued close cooperation in our endeavor to relax tensions and to venture peaceful co-existence.

In your report, Mr. President, you enumerated three principles essential in building up a structure of peace: partnership, strength, and willingness to negotiate. My Government wholeheartedly endorses these principles. It will use its best endeavors to bear its due share to the full extent.

As between our two nations, partnership holds paramount

93

rank for us. It is founded not only on common interests, but even more so on common beliefs.

It is in the spirit of this partnership that I ask you to raise your glasses and join me in proposing a toast to the happiness of the American people, to the friendship between our two nations, to your health, Mrs. Nixon, and to the health of the President of the United States.

25

Address by Chancellor Brandt at Harvard University on June 5, 1972, Twenty-Five Years After the Announcement of the Marshall Plan

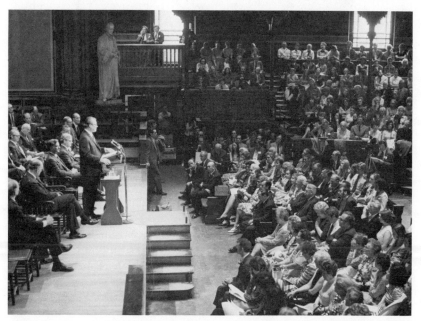

Chancellor Brandt delivering address at Harvard University commemorating the 25th anniversary of the Marshall Plan, Cambridge, Mass., June 5, 1972.

Chancellor Brandt announced in his address to Harvard University the creation of a "German Marshall Fund of the U.S." It was at Harvard University twenty-five years earlier that American Secretary of State George Marshall had proclaimed his European Recovery Program:

History does not too often give us occasion to speak of fortunate events. But here in this place a quarter of a century ago an event took place which could rightly be termed one of the strokes of providence of this century, a century which has not so very often been illuminated by the light of reason.

We are gathered here at this ceremony to commemorate the speech with which George Marshall announced 25 years ago a plan which was to become one of America's most formidable and most successful achievements. I have no authority to speak for any country other than my own, but I know, and I want the American people to know that our gratitude, the gratitude of Europeans, lives on. What we give in return is our growing ability to be a partner of the United States and in addition, apart from regulating our own affairs, to assume our share of responsibility in the world at large.

To go back to the beginning: if happiness is a concept in which mankind perceives an objective, then in our epoch it has for long stretches remained in the shadow. The era of my generation was a concentration of more darkness, more bitterness and more suffering than nations have ever before brought upon themselves. Against this background, the act we are commemorating here today shines brilliantly.

The Toll Of Two World Wars

Two world wars, which were first and foremost civil wars in Europe, plunged our civilization into the abyss of self-destruction. Ten million times in the first, more than fifty million times in the second catastrophe, one individual and irreplaceable human life was destroyed—on the battlefield, in air-raid shelters, in camps, by firing squads, in the gas chambers, or by sheer starvation.

And the most depressing part of it is that this century is laden with the stigma of names that have become the ciphers of ruin, names denoting the nameless ravaging of souls, and that tell us that hell on earth was a reality. We have known since then that man is capable of revolting collectively against any moral commandment and of surrendering that quality for which he was born: his ability to be human.

We cannot and do not want to shake off this experience nor our awareness of the threat that accompanies us day by day in the form of the multiplication of the means of destruction capable of snuffing out our whole civilization if they slip from our control. If we are no longer the master of that difficult peace we have today, that peace which we regard as our day-to-day task but also as the *ultima ratio* of our existence. For this we have learned (as I said six months ago in Oslo): war has become the *ultima irratio* of this century.

A Soldier's Act Of Peace

There are many who had forethoughts of this. One of them was George Catlett Marshall. He was a soldier. In other words, he served a profession which presupposes constant readiness for war with all its consequences. I put it plainly because it brings into even greater relief the exemplary achievement of this man. That achievement was underlined by the award of the Nobel Prize for Peace.

He was a soldier out of passion. But this word has a double meaning. In this case it is the passion and energy with which Marshall discharged the duties of his profession. It also includes his readiness to suffer and to share the suffering of others, a quality indispensable in a good soldier and man of character.

As a young staff officer charged with complicated strategic and logistical duties, he witnessed the first mass loss of life at St. Mihiel and in the Argonne Forest in France in 1917 and 1918. We know that this experience marked his life. It did not cause him to falter in the steadiness of purpose which characterized the stages in his career during the interval of that precarious peace between the cease-fire of Compiègne and the 1st of September 1939—that 1st of September when the German attack was launched against Poland and when George Marshall became Chief of Staff of the United States Army.

Acting upon the instructions of his President, he took steps to ensure that the United States was heavily armed in its neutrality. Yet it was clear to him that America would be challenged for a second time to decide Europe's destiny. He was known as the organizer of victory. His circumspection and his exact yet imaginative strategy were the mathematics of the campaigns and battles upon which the Third Reich and the crazed policies of its leaders crumbled.

1945 Different From 1918

The end was bitter, and not only for the vanquished. Victories, too, can be bitter, especially if they carry the seed for future conflicts as in 1918, when the war was won, and peace was lost for want of reason on the part of the winners and the losers, through stubborn mistrust on the one side, through resentment of the humiliated on the other. Against the wish of its President, the United States left Europe to itself, left it prone to the animosities and jealousies born of national pride which did not cease to exist when the nations laid down their arms.

At that time America's political and military leaders, faithful to the traditions of their fathers, felt that their duty was to withdraw and abstain from further international involvement. But, in fact it was no longer possible and apparently no longer permissible.

It was different in 1945. George Marshall and others agreed that victory did not relieve his country of its responsibility. The United States did not for a moment claim that responsibility for itself. It shared it with its allies, in particular with Britain, which in 1940, putting up a lone resistance, refused to surrender its freedom. And with France, who, despite being sorely wounded, picked herself up again. But not least with the Soviet Union, which had fought tenaciously and suffered particularly heavy losses, and which now found the door to Central Europe thrown open as a result of Hitler's war.

The understanding between the big powers called for their joint exercise of responsibility. But even before the war was over, the victorious powers quarreled over who should exercise influence over the liberated countries. Defeated Germany then became both the cause and the object of the cold war. For a second time it seemed that hardly had the fighting stopped, than peace was lost in the clash of power interests and ideological conflict.

Constructive Answer From U.S.

In that desperate situation President Harry Truman recalled General Marshall from retirement and appointed him Secretary of State on January 21, 1947. Not as Chief of Staff for the Cold War, as many might have feared, but as the man who, having organized the war, was now looked upon to organize peace.

The world hoped for and expected a constructive answer from the United States to the challenge of despair, helplessness and distress. The will to live had not become extinct in the hearts of the nations of Europe. Creative spirits on both sides of the Atlantic, who realized that no more time should be lost, had long been at work in providing that answer. The plan which bears the name of George Marshall was forged from many ideas and suggestions. Sober analysis of the absurd situation in Europe after the Moscow Conference of April, 1947 converged with the determination to act before that terrible "too late" could be uttered.

The European Recovery Program which the Secretary of State outlined here 25 years ago contained a sincere offer to restore collective East-West responsibility for Europe. The East rejected that offer, and that meant the widening and cementing of division. As you know, in those days I was in Berlin and I say quite openly here that Ernst Reuter and I did not find it easy to recognize this painful reality. We deplored the division of the continent, of our country, of our own city. We could not cede our will for unity to the advocates of nationalistic protest. But we did not want to give up the chance afforded by our regained freedom. We had to pit our will to assert ourselves against the danger of paralysis.

Berlin As Focal Point

Berlin became the cradle of German-American friendship. The refusal to resign itself to the situation became the basis for future partnership. At the same time, the help we received to help ourselves could only benefit the countries of Western Europe, and that became a turning point in international relations.

In speaking of this assistance, I do not overlook the help given in various ways by private charitable organizations, who commenced their activities even before the hostilities were over. I cannot emphasize too highly the moral support which came from their assistance then and in future years.

The Marshall Plan mobilized American reserves to provide Western Europe with the capital and raw materials it needed to regain its vitality. That program explicitly included defeated Germany. It was not only the magnanimity that is part of America's nature, and not only the willingness to help which is characteristic of the people of this country, that inspired the leaders of the most powerful nation in the world to come to the aid of the defeated. It was, of course, also a political calculation which looked beyond the current state of affairs to the horizons of coming decades. By this I mean more than that America understandably thought about its position in relation to the Soviet Union: I mean, above all, that the Marshall Plan challenged the European partners to enter into close economic cooperation. Inherent in the Plan was also an appeal for a common political course.

This was the basic element of the program which I say without hesitation bears the mark of genius. It traced, though tentatively, the aim of European, or at least West European, unity. It was more than the release of economic dynamism, more than the rekindling of industrial vitality which produced miracles not only in the Federal Republic of Germany after the currency reform. Every nation of Western Europe showed in its own way that it possessed the unbroken will to work and pull itself up again, a will that had only waited to be sparked.

Europe's Self-Confidence Renewed

With his Plan, George Marshall roused Europe's stifled self-confidence. He gave many citizens of the old continent a concrete stimulus to bring down from the stars the vision of a Europe united in lasting peace. The first step towards that aim was the OEEC, the Organization for European Economic Cooperation. Progressive thinkers in France, Italy, the Netherlands, Britain and Germany were prepared for this change. The most outstanding among them was Jean Monnet. He was, in fact, Marshall's partner in Europe. The great Frenchman and European saw more clearly than others the need for modern economic planning on a wide scale, an asset that was partly attributable to his precise knowledge of the American reality. He knew that national frontiers had to be removed or at least made bridgeable if the Continent was to be revitalized.

The Schuman Plan, which by merging the coal and steel industries in the Western part of our Continent was a significant first step to the joint organization of its economic energies, was inspired by this great man. His progressive determination coincided with the realistic instinct of three conservative statesmen whose European consciousness was embedded in a historical fold that lay deeper than the ideal of the nation-state: Robert Schuman, Konrad Adenauer and Alcide de Gasperi.

Marshall Plan, OEEC and the Coal and Steel Community— and concurrently the cessation of a negative occupation policy as manifest in the dismantling of industry—were the first stageposts of that European renaissance, a term I prefer to the "German miracle" which really was a European one.

This leads us to ponder a little more the ties that link America inseparably with the destiny of the old Continent. It was James Monroe who said that the new world would restore the equilibrium of the old. He has been proved right—in spite of the latent isolationist tendencies in America that are sometimes traced back to his doctrine. When he spoke of this equilibrium he anticipated the reality we aspire to through transatlantic partnership.

Equal Responsibilities

In one of his early political writings, Thomas Mann described the Atlantic as the "new Mediterranean" and ascribed to the nation on this side of the ocean the legacy of ancient Rome. Ingenious comparisons of this kind fire our imagination; yet we are conscious of their dubiousness. Nowhere has the United States been prescribed an imperial destiny along classical lines, and past decades have proved that Europe, contrary to all the pessimistic oracles, was by no means doomed for decline as ancient Greece.

On the contrary: the Marshall Plan was productive proof that America needs a self-confident Europe capable of forming a common political will. The United States is waiting for us Europeans to create the institutions capable of acting in our joint name. It waits for Europe to grow into an equal partner with whom it can share the burden of responsibility for world affairs. We are patiently trying to do this by seeking to enlarge and develop the Community which, now with the inclusion of Britain, Ireland, Denmark and Norway, is in the process of creating an economic and monetary union and of establishing closer political cooperation.

I may add that America's impatience over the slow progress being made in this direction is to some extent understandable. But that impatience was based on the wrong premise; it was erroneous to believe that Europe could reproduce what had become a reality in the United States.

In Europe, the idea was not to level off national entities but rather to preserve their identities while combining their energies to form a new whole. The idea was, and still is, to organize Europe in such a way that it will remain European.

Yet, however tightly Western Europe may grow together, America will not be able to sever its European links. It will not be able to forget that the Western part of the Old World will remain an area of vital interest to it, a relevant conclusion reached by Walter Lippmann from his fifty years' experience as a critical observer of world affairs.

Cooperation With The East

The nations of East and South East Europe, in spite of their less favorable starting position and conditions, have also given an impressive performance of reconstruction and modernization. Thus we should not underestimate the possibilities for cooperation across the whole of Europe that may arise in the years ahead. Are we, after all, not now progressing beyond our bilateral experiences towards a conference on security and cooperation in Europe with the participation of the United States and Canada? And though euphoria would be quite out of place in this connection it would be unwise not to take any opportunity that holds out the prospect of success, however slight.

It is general knowledge that the Federal Republic of Germany is endeavoring to contribute in its own specific way to the improvement of relations and to the consolidation of peace in Europe. But our policy of conciliation and understanding with Eastern Europe could not for one moment mean that Europe and the United States would move apart. On the contrary: the will for detente is a joint program of the Atlantic Alliance.

With the treaties of Moscow and Warsaw, to which several other agreements will be added, the Federal Republic of Germany has not only honored its pledge to seek reconciliation, in which we see a moral duty, it has in fact returned after a period of unclarity to the mainstream of the will of the world, which commands East and West to relax cramped positions and ease the permanent strain of the cold war. In pursuing this aim we have never lost sight of the dictates of security, including military security.

Atlantic Alliance Is Basis

The Atlantic Community has truly acquired a new dynamism. It has developed into the entity prescribed for it by its founders: an Alliance for peace, an Alliance both militarily prepared and capable of negotiating without cherishing illusions. The Alliance remains the basis of our plans and of our actions. Its reliability has encouraged our French and British friends, and ourselves, to remind our neighbors in the East that behind the barriers of power interest and spheres of influence, behind the ineffaceable delimitations of ideological differences, behind the irreconcilability of social concepts, there waits the new reality of a larger Europe which should be capable of harmonizing its interests under the banner of peace.

Our parliamentary debate over the treaties of Moscow and Warsaw was hard. It has shown that the process of détente can only be enhanced by a steadfast and sober policy. Our courage to accept realities should express itself in this sobriety: a sense of reality which other nations have too often found lacking in the Germans. We need this sense of reality more urgently than ever before, because liquidating the cold war really means closing the accounts on the Second World War.

Europe And America

In this phase of change, America's presence in Europe is more necessary the ever. I trust that those who carry responsibility in this country will not refuse to appreciate this. American-European partnership is indispensable if America does not want to neglect its own interests and if our Europe is to forge itself into a productive system instead of again becoming a volcanic terrain of crisis, anxiety and confusion.

The forms of the American commitment may change, but an actual disengagement would cancel out a basic law of our peace. It would be tantamount to abdication. We want our American friends to know, however, that we have viewed with anything but indifference the heavy external and internal burdens which they have had to carry during this period. The fact that America does not depress its critical problems but faces up to them unsparingly is in our eyes proof of its unbroken strength. And the fact that it does not take them lightly does not weaken but rather increases our sympathy and the reliability of our partnership.

1947 marked the beginning of the Cold War, not because but in spite of the Marshall Plan. The situation resulting from the cold war is one of the bitter realities with which America, like Europe, still has to contend today. The results of the Marshall Plan have

among other things enabled us twenty-five years after its procla-
mation to embark on a policy which has made 1972 a year that
may one day also be regarded as a turning-point in world politics.

President Nixon has signed agreements with the leaders of
the Soviet Union intended to reduce confrontation and to mark
clearly the areas of cooperation. Europe in particular can only
benefit from the introduction of stabilizing factors in the relations
between the two superpowers, which lead to greater security.

President Nixon has rightly attributed worldwide significance to the Quadripartite Agreement on Berlin which entered into
force two days ago. It is the result of a great common achievement
that West Berlin has been able to survive all the crises of a quarter
of a century and that now, its link with the Federal Republic being
no longer in question, it can look to a secure future.

This also means—and this is a fact not yet appreciated anywhere—that the presence of the United States in the center of
Europe, unlimited in point of time, has been confirmed with the
consent of the Soviet Union.

Reduction Of Arms

Moreover one of our greatest tasks in the years ahead will be not
to increase but to limit, and where possible to reduce, the mightiest
destructive potential that ever was on the soil of Europe, and to do
so on both sides, in East and West. If we can together limit our
armaments—mutually and balanced—instead of building up our
arsenals in a race against each other there may be perspectives
opened up that will lead to cooperation between East and West
in Europe.

If we can now carefully prepare a conference on security and
cooperation in Europe it is an expression of the reality that the
United States will participate as a power without which there can
be no security in Europe. To have recognized this reality is an
important contribution by the Soviet leaders.

By dint of hard work, and with American support, Western
Europe is now back on its own feet. With the aid of the United
States, it has again found its own personality. Thus we in Europe,
and especially we in the Federal Republic, are deeply indebted to
this country.

But in this hour let us not only look backwards. Let the
memory of the past become our mission of the future, let us accept
the new challenge and perceive the new opportunity: peace through
cooperation.

Let me stress once again that to build this structure we need
the United States, its commitment, its guarantee and its cooperation.

It is precisely now that we need increasing understanding for our partners on both sides of the Atlantic. The Federal Republic of Germany wishes to help bring this about. It is the expression of our special gratitude for the American decision in 1947 not to keep us out. It is an expression of our conviction that we can achieve peace only jointly and by cooperation.

German Marshall Plan Memorial

On the occasion of the 25th anniversary of the announcement of the European Recovery Program by Secretary of State George Marshall, we, my colleagues representing all parties of our Parliament and I, wish to inform you of several measures taken by the Federal Republic of Germany with a view to closer understanding between partners on both sides of the Atlantic in the 1970s and 80s.

1. The German Federal Government has established the financial basis for the setting up of a German Marshall Plan Memorial in the United States. A fund has meanwhile been incorporated and constituted in the District of Columbia as an independent American Foundation: "The German Marshall Fund of the United States—A Memorial to the Marshall Plan." Its by-laws have been adopted, its board members and officers elected.

   The Federal Government undertakes to provide the Fund with 150 million Deutschmarks to be paid over the next fifteen years in installments of 10 million Deutschmarks due on June 5th each year. All parties represented in the German Bundestag approved the Government's appropriation bill for these funds.

   Under the arrangements made between the German Government and the Fund's Board of Directors, the German Marshall Fund will administer its proceeds without any influence by German authorities, and will use them to promote American European study and research projects.

   There will be three main areas on which the Fund will concentrate its interest:

   (a) the comparative study of problems confronting advanced industrial societies in Europe, North America and other parts of the world;
   (b) the study of problems of international relations that pertain to the common interests of Europe and the United States;
   (c) support for the field of European studies.

2. Upon the suggestion of the Federal Government, the program of West European Studies of Harvard University will receive this year a non-recurring grant of three million Deutschmarks from the German Marshall Fund to establish a "German Marshall

Memorial Endowment" for the promotion of European study projects.

3. The German Government has always attached special significance to exchanges with the United States in the field of science. This is also reflected in the consistent support it has given the German-American Fulbright Program. So as to make it more effective, the German Government has decided to increase its financial contribution substantially above the amount expected of it as a matching contribution—from the present two million to three and a half million Deutschmarks per year.

4. In order to improve cooperation in specialized fields between American and German research institutes, the German Government has adopted a sponsorship program for the exchange of highly-qualified American and German scientists. The German Ministry of Education and Science will earmark five million Deutschmarks per year for this exchange program.

5. The Donors' Association for German Science, an institution established by German industrial and commercial firms, has undertaken to replenish by two and a half million Deutschmarks a year the amount made available by the Federal Government for the sponsorship program. These additional funds will be used for exchanges of scholars in the field of the humanities.

We in the Federal Republic of Germany hope that these measures will have a beneficial effect on our partnership. And thus we follow up on the will for common effort that characterized the Marshall Plan Program.

Above all, we want to arouse in the younger generation that mutual trust which in those days exhorted the Europeans to make peace among themselves. They must not forget that the interdependence of states on both sides of the Atlantic proclaimed by John F. Kennedy must remain a moral, a cultural, an economic and a political reality. It must not be renounced, nor must it be weakened. It is part of the as yet unwritten constitution of the future Europe which we continue to strive for: with gratitude and respect for the man whose work we commemorate here today, the soldier who saw his life's fulfillment in an act for peace. Twenty-five years ago he recruited us in the service of peace. In the spirit of his aims we shall endeavor to do our duty.

Mr. President, ladies and gentlemen, I am pleased that we have with us here today the Chairman of the Board of the German Marshall Fund of the United States, Dean Harvey Brooks, as well as the Chairman of the Board of Overseers of Harvard University and Chairman of the Fund's Honorary Committee, Mr. C. Douglas Dillon.

It is my honor and privilege to ask them to accept the deeds by which the German Government sets up the German Marshall Fund of the United States and the German Marshall Memorial Endowment of Harvard's Program for West European Studies, together with the checks for the first of the fifteen annual installments.

26

Exchange of Remarks Between President Ford and Chancellor Schmidt, December 5, 1974

Chancellor Helmut Schmidt paid his first official visit to the United States December 4–12, 1974. Following is the exchange of remarks between President Gerald Ford and the West German Chancellor:

The President: Chancellor Schmidt, gentlemen:

I am delighted to welcome you here in Washington, our Nation's Capital, on behalf of the American people.

This is your first visit, Mr. Chancellor, to the United States as the leader of the German Federal Government. It comes at an historic time for both of our countries.

We, in the United States, are on the eve of our Bicentennial. One of the things that we are particularly aware of is the prominent role played by men and women of German descent in the building of America over the past two centuries. They have made tremendous contributions in fields as widespread as education and science, culture and the arts.

A few months ago the Federal Republic of Germany marked its own 25th anniversary. During this quarter century, the Federal Republic has become one of the world's leading political and economic powers, and also one of its most responsible.

Throughout this entire period of relations between our two countries, it has been marked by a very close friendship and a very close cooperation, and we are particularly proud of that association.

Mr. Chancellor, we live in demanding times. In the effort to solve the formidable economic and political problems confronting us today, close cooperation and mutual help have become infinitely more important than ever. Only by working together can we overcome the current difficulties facing our economies and international economy.

I believe we can do it, and speaking for the American people, I appreciate the support your Government has shown for strengthened economic cooperation in the international field.

We also recognize your international contributions in dealing with the problems of energy, food, and financial pressures.

A keystone, of course, of our present and future cooperation is the Atlantic Alliance. At a time when all members of the Alliance confront budgetary difficulties, difficult choices for all of them, we applaud and endorse your country's positive attitude toward maintaining the strength of NATO.

We also appreciate, Mr. Chancellor, your cooperation in helping to assure that no nation bear an unfair burden of the cost of our common defense.

We will have many important issues to discuss today and tomorrow, Mr. Chancellor. I look forward to those discussions in full confidence that these talks will contribute significantly to our efforts in creating more stable political and economic conditions throughout the world. I know that your visit will further strengthen the already close friendship and partnership between the Federal Republic and the United States.

Mr. Chancellor, America bids you and your party a most cordial welcome.

The Chancellor. Mr. President, ladies and gentlemen:

Thank you, Mr. President, very much for your warm welcome and for the kind words, regardful words addressed to me and my party.

As you have said, this is not my first visit to the United States, but the first time that I have come to this country as the head of government of the Federal Republic of Germany.

I am particularly glad to have this opportunity so soon after you, Mr. President, have assumed your office in order to exchange views on the main questions which do concern us both.

In today's world, we are faced with a multitude of difficult problems whose solutions will make unprecedented demands on our countries and will require us to harness our strength in the common effort.

The world is threatened by severe economic disruption. The Middle East conflict, whose settlement your Administration is working so hard to bring about, and the energy crisis, which followed in its wake, have suddenly opened our eyes to the fragile nature of the foundations on which our economic and social and political stability does rest.

The strengthening of these foundations is a task which does concern us all and which we can only master through broad international cooperation, as you said.

We, in Germany, are conscious of this challenge, and we are preparing ourselves to meet it. In this search we do attach specific importance to close cooperation and consultation between the United States of America and Europe and my own country.

The partnership between the United States and Europe has stood the test. It has existed for more than 25 years in the Atlantic Alliance, which was strengthened by the Declaration of Ottawa in the middle of this year. It has also reflected our common efforts to promote détente in Europe and in the world.

We are resolved to do everything within our capability to strengthen and to further develop this partnership.

The untroubled friendship between the United States and the Federal Republic of Germany seems to be an excellent basis for this, and it is my firm conviction that our meeting, Mr. President, will bring us closer to this goal.

Thank you very much.

27

Visit of President Scheel to the United States, June 16, 1975

President Scheel and President Ford conferring at the White House, Washington, during state visit to the United States June 15–20, 1975.

After Theodor Heuss, Walter Scheel was the second Federal President to make an official visit to the United States. Following are the welcoming statement by President Ford and President Scheel's response:

President Ford. Mr. President, ladies and gentlemen:

It is a very great honor and a personal pleasure, Mr. President, to welcome you here on behalf of the American people. Although this is your first visit as a Federal President, you have been welcomed to our country on many previous occasions. I, therefore, greet you not only as Federal President but also as an old and very dear friend of America.

Over 17 years have passed since your distinguished predecessor, Theodor Heuss, paid us a state visit. In that year, 1958, the

110

Federal Republic was in the early stages of a remarkable economic recovery and growth, which can now be seen as an economic miracle. The Federal Republic was on its way to becoming one of our strongest allies, one of our most important trading partners and closest of friends.

We have seen many, many changes since the late 1950's. Mr. President, today we face new challenges of unparalleled complexity, including those of energy and international economics. Yet, the basic principles of our foreign policies and of our relationship remain sound and constant.

We are as strongly committed as we were 17 years ago to safeguarding the freedom of the West. We have remained committed to the freedom and security of Berlin. We see the peace and security of Central Europe as a true test of the process known as détente.

Only a few days ago I made my first visit to Europe as President of the United States. In Brussels, the heads of government of the North Atlantic nations met and reaffirmed the continuing solidarity of our Alliance and the continuing strength of our commitment to the goals that unite our peoples.

In the era now before us, I can say with confidence that Americans are committed to this Alliance with renewed dedication, vision, and purpose.

It is my intention, Mr. President, to work in close concert with you to serve our peoples' common objectives. Together, our strong, free, and prosperous nations can achieve much for our own peoples and for mankind.

Your visit, Mr. President, bears eloquent testimony to the friendship and partnership of the Federal Republic of Germany and the United States. In this spirit, I bid you a most cordial welcome on this occasion, and I look forward to our discussions of the problems of mutual interest and concern.

President Scheel. Mr. President, Mrs. Ford:

My wife and I should like to express our sincere thanks for your friendly words of welcome.

Today, I come to the White House for the first time as President of the Federal Republic of Germany. What is, after all, the purpose of such a state visit?

Firstly, by its very character, it is intended to mirror the state of mutual relations. These relations are, I know of no doubt about it, excellent. We are showing people both at home and abroad how close are the ties which unite us. This is a good thing, and important, too. It is something the world should—indeed must—know.

Such a visit also enables us to take stock. We look back at the past. The bicentenary of the founding of the United States is near at hand. The 30th anniversary of the end of the war in Europe is just over. Both anniversaries play an important part in our relations.

The United States Constitution gave birth to modern democracy based on freedom, and thus to the democratic family of nations to which the Federal Republic also belongs.

For us Germans, the 30th anniversary of the end of the war calls forth ambivalent feelings, but it also reminds us of the debt of gratitude we owe to the people of the United States for the generous help they afforded their former enemy. I need not press the point that this help will never be forgotten.

But we must not only dwell on the past; we must also face up to the present. No one, Mr. President, has a clearer picture than you and the Government you lead of the problems of worldwide dimensions which confront us today.

The free Western World has taken up this historic challenge. I am convinced it has enough courage, perception, imagination, and initiative to solve the pending problems.

Of course, this cannot be done unless we join forces. Alone, everyone for himself, we shall not succeed. This means that we need European unification. We need the Atlantic partnership between a united Europe and the United States of America.

This Atlantic partnership must comprise not only our common security policy, which will continue to be vital, but also all political spheres of importance for both sides. In particular, it must include a common approach to the crucial economic and monetary problems facing the world today. Every step towards more solidarity, I believe, is a step to strengthening our free democratic system.

Your impressive visit to Europe underlined once more these fundamental truths. The countries joined in the Atlantic partnership do not cut themselves off from the outside world. Indeed, one of the reasons for uniting has been to contribute with our combined strengths towards a solution of the global social problem of our time—that of development.

The chances for the survival of democracy are, as I see it, crucially dependent on the forces of freedom all over the world, finding the right answer to this problem.

Mr. President, I am pleased to feel that I am a welcome guest in your country. Let me say here and now that you, too, would be a highly welcome guest in our country. I do hope that I will be able in the not too distant future to welcome you in Bonn as the guest of the Federal Republic of Germany. But right now, Mr. President, I am looking forward to my talks with you.

Thank you.

President Ford.

Thank you very much. I look forward to coming there.

28

President Scheel's Address Before Congress,
June 17, 1975

President Scheel addressing the U.S. Congress, Washington, June 17, 1975. Behind President Scheel: Vice President Rockefeller and House Speaker Albert.

Following an introduction by the Speaker of the House, President Scheel addressed a joint meeting of the two houses of Congress:

Mr. President, Mr. Speaker, you have invited me to address you. I appreciate this special gesture. I respond by expressing the deep respect which every democrat owes to this outstanding assembly. I am glad of this opportunity to express some thoughts on questions that are of concern to all people in the free world.

The world is fraught with unrest and problems, and I am grateful to be able to discuss them with you.

Today all governments with a sense of responsibility unavoidably find themselves competing to save mankind from misery and anarchy. The leaders in that contest are not automatically the powerful ones, but rather those who can come up with convincing answers to the problems of modern society.

We have had to learn that not only the individual is mortal but the whole of mankind. It can perish in a few days through arms of destruction. It can perish in a few generations through environmental pollution and the wasteful exploitation of its natural resources.

The words of St. Matthew still hold true for the whole of mankind. No town, no household that is divided against itself can stand. The community in this situation has nothing more to fear than the passions of egotism. It needs nothing more than the voice of reason which reconciles the different elements and forges them into a whole. That voice has often been raised on this side of the Atlantic. When Europe began to break up the old feudal systems with new democratic ideas, the American Revolution turned the theory of democracy into practice.

When the nations of Europe picked themselves up from the debris in 1945, it was the United States who through its inspired leadership galvanized the forces of the old continent into a coordinated recovery operation.

That action was perhaps the most generous in the history of mankind. It will be associated forever with the name of Secretary of State George Marshall.

My country was included in it as early as 1947. Indeed in 1946 already a great American statesman, Secretary of State James Byrnes, in his historic speech in Stuttgart held out a hand to the former enemy. The tests and dangers we had withstood together let this understanding grow into a well-tried political partnership. That partnership has rendered us capable of great achievements. It has made our ostpolitik possible and has enabled us to defuse the complex and dangerous Berlin problem.

But the freedom of Berlin is not based on international agreements alone. Berlin remains free by virtue of deeds ever since American citizens risked, indeed, sacrificed, their lives during the airlift. It remained free by virtue of the words by which President Kennedy called himself a "Berliner." That city remains a decisive hinge of East-West relations in Europe. Here the strengths of any policy of détente and our alliance are put to the test day by day.

It is true, I speak to you as the representative of a divided nation. We have not succeeded in overcoming the artificial and unnatural division of Germany by peaceful means. Other than peaceful means have never been thought up, nor will they be. No one will understand better than you, Senators and Congressmen, that a nation can never forego its unity as a political goal.

115

The first essential is this: If a rational and sincere policy of détente is to have any meaning for us, it must surely be to make it easier for the people in divided Germany to live together.

After the darkest years in our history, the United States gave us generous support. But let me also say that nothing of what you have done for us since has been in vain. You have gained a good ally who makes its full contribution toward the defense capability of the alliance, a contribution that is second to none but that of the United States. An ally for democracy, a partner for the efforts which Europe and America will have to make together in order to enable all people to live in conditions worthy of man.

But the partners of the Atlantic Alliance who include the oldest democracies on Earth must not shirk the question, "Can our democratic way of life survive?" Has it not already been overtaken by the accelerating rate of change in the world? Do we still have the moral strength to find for ourselves and others the way through the uncertain?

These questions lead us back to the ideas of which our democracies were born.

I am convinced that they will stand scrutiny. They make us alive to the reliable, the constant elements of our policy; the Atlantic Alliance on which our freedom and our freedom of action rests and the common values in which our partnership is rooted.

The meeting of the NATO Council in Brussels and the prominent role which President Ford played there have concurred that these are joint beliefs and vital links. The political responsibility of the world power America extends beyond the Atlantic area. Wherever world peace is threatened, this country places its enormous weight on the scales of peace. And at this present time as well the world hopes that the courage and perseverance of its political leaders will give them the strength to forge peace in the Middle East bit by bit. For what use are the dignity and freedom of man if they lack the ground of peace in which to grow?

Belief in these very values, the dignity and freedom of man, has inspired our best political minds for over two centuries. When my own generation entered upon the political scene, we considered the model offered by America as proof that the concept of Western democracy was a fitting basis from which to cope with the problems of this, the most difficult of all worlds.

I realize that for 12 years those ideals were treated with shocking contempt in Germany, and yet freedom ultimately prevailed. Exactly 22 years ago today, on the 17th of June 1953, it showed its elemental strength when East Berlin workers, heedless of the risks to life and limb, hoisted the black, red, and gold flag on the Brandenburg Gate.

Totalitarianism may use arbitrary means, yet in the end freedom will triumph. Nevertheless, freedom can preserve its strength only if each generation anew makes it its own. In the European Community democratic forces openly vie with one another and with the Communists, but we have learned that our idea of freedom will be cogent only as long as it is the motive force of social change. If this is not so, it remains a hollow word.

The catchword of our time is "détente." It is a fundamental objective of our foreign policy. It is a great hope of our Nation. But the peaceful existence side by side of East and West knows of no cease-fire on the ideological front. And the fronts in this ideological battle run right through the German nation, which has been divided for decades. We shall be the losers in that struggle unless we see why Communist ideologies are effective in Europe or in the Third World. We see Communism succeed where injustice and misery predominate, and we have to sharpen our conscience.

It is my belief that political freedom cannot prevail where the social conscience remains silent. In our two countries we have been able to humanize working conditions without revolution and bloodshed. Our political leaders have rated human dignity and freedom higher than the rights of the powerful in the free market. They know that political freedom becomes a farce unless the individual has the material means of self-realization. Freedom and social justice go together. Social peace is the prerequisite for a nation's inner strength. Without that inner strength it has no strength internationally.

Our Constitution upholds the concept of ownership as the basis of a free economic order. But at the same time, it postulates the social obligation inherent in ownership. That is what our Constitution, the basic law of the Federal Republic of Germany, prescribes, and this has been the approach of all governments of the Federal Republic of Germany.

Ten million refugees from the lost regions of Eastern Germany found a new homeland in the destroyed and overpopulated western part of our country. Generous legislation and the sacrifices made by the people gave those expellees equal opportunities. My country is proud of that achievement.

Today we are trying to achieve a balance of interests and opportunities on a much larger scale. The entire world economic order must be given the chance to develop further, but in the process nothing should be given up that has proved its value.

We are called upon to share responsibility for answering vital questions from five continents: Tomorrow's grain and rice deficit, the interplay of population pressure and economic development, the mounting cost of military security. The starving in many parts of the world still need our help. Young nations who hoped to achieve industrial prosperity overnight with the aid of our capital and technology are disappointed and put the blame on us. The industrialized countries can only meet these challenges if their economic constitution is sound.

This means for our countries we must continue along the paths we have taken in fighting unemployment and worldwide recession. Our economic policies must give sufficient impulses to domestic demand.

One thing is certain. Only through close cooperation between North America and Europe, and by harmonizing interests, have we any prospect of mastering such tasks. It is certain that our combined energies will not provide the solution without the contributions of other nations. And it is certain also that we would be betraying the old fundamental ideas of democracy if we were always to be found on the side of those who defend property and privilege against social demands, demands born of hunger and distress.

It is our task to find evolutionary solutions, but this is no easy matter. The welfare of our peoples which we have to guard did not come to us overnight. We owe it to the hard work and privations of whole generations. It would be politically meaningless and economically impossible just to transfer our assets and our social achievements to others, as some developing countries would like it.

Our aim is not to maintain the status quo, but to seek harmonization of interests. The readiness to accept change is the prerequisite for the pursuit of happiness, and in that context it is the spirit we adopt in our relations with the partners from other camps that will be decisive. Our diplomatic tools shall not include threats and intimidation. In a spirit of partnership, without mental reservation, it is possible to reconcile even sharply conflicting interests. In everything we do we must start from the fact that in the decades ahead there is only one rational course open to us, that of cooperation.

The nine European states have, with much good will, worked out an overall modus of economic cooperation with the nations of Africa, Asia, and the Caribbean. In protracted negotiations, sharply differing points of view and interests of many sovereign partners have been harmonized. Here we have a promising example of multilateral cooperation with the Third World. It also shows that the European community can have a stabilizing influence on the world economy.

At the same time, it becomes clear that the European community is capable of helping to ease the burden of the United States, once it finds its way to joint action. The European union to which we have committed ourselves has not yet been completed, and to be frank, in this respect we are still a long way behind our hopes and our promises. But Europe is needed, and we shall build it, and in so doing, we need the understanding of the United States.

We need long-term European-American cooperation. It must be based on mutual trust. It must be candid. It must not again make the mistake of emphasizing divergent secondary interests at the expense of primary common interests. We need not only the willpower and the technical capability of the United States which President Ford referred to in Brussels but also, to quote him again, "its spiritual drive and steadiness of purpose." Not as some may have feared and others may have hoped, recent developments have not loosened the ties of European-American solidarity. On the contrary, more energies have been set free for the alliance which will be concentrated on its tasks. The awareness of our interdependence is deeper than ever. It has above all become clear to us that it is the common fundamental democratic beliefs which distinguished the alliance from others and which nourished its strength in each member state.

I believe in a Europe committed to the human rights that were embodied for the first time in the constitution of Massachusetts, a Europe which fills these principles with a sense of social justice of our generation. Only with a deeper understanding of our spiritual heritage will the democracies on either side of the North Atlantic be able to assert themselves and thus effectively serve the cause of world peace.

Together with you, we shall recall the concepts and ideals of the American Revolution. May our age find us as resolved, as realistic, but also as idealistic as those men and women who made this great country.

29

Exchange of Toasts Between President Ford and President Scheel, July 27, 1975

President Ford visited the Federal Republic of Germany July 26–28. During a dinner cruise on the Rhine River the following toasts were exchanged between President Ford and President Scheel:

President Scheel. Mr. President, Mrs. Ford, ladies and gentlemen:

A few weeks ago at the splendid reception before the White House in Washington, I expressed the wish to soon be able to greet you here in Germany. To my delight, the international conference calendar has helped to make this wish come true so soon.

Today you are here. I bid you, Mrs. Ford, and your associates a warm welcome. You do know that you are highly appreciated and highly welcome guests in our country.

We know, ladies and gentlemen, that wherever the President of the United States goes in the world, his office follows him—the White House. My house has the color in common with yours. It is white, undoubtedly. However, it is too small to accommodate a festive party in your honor. This is why I invited you to this white boat.

Outside the banks are gliding by—things are in motion like the river. We may have been cruising against the current. We have just turned around. At any rate, the further we go together on this truly European stream, the brighter the views.

This corresponds to a political hope and to a political goal. It is our hope, it is our goal to create a solidly founded, strong Europe which, together with the United States of America, will secure a future of peace and freedom.

The closer we come to Europe, the brighter the prospects. Much has been achieved. The British people have clearly and for good decided in favor of Europe. European political cooperation has pointed up new possibilities to develop Europe institutionally. Yet much remains to be done.

All Western countries are struggling with economic problems at the present. But more and more, the view is gaining ground that individual countries by themselves cannot master these difficulties.

The talks which the Federal Government has conducted in the course of these past days make it clear that the willingness to make common efforts is on the rise.

Europe is moving in the direction of coordinating its different economic policies. This is another important step towards progress. Out of these very difficulties we gain insights and strengths to overcome these difficulties.

Europe by itself will not be able to master the economic problems of today. We can only be successful if we coordinate our efforts with those of the United States of America, and this cannot but strengthen the awareness of the benefits and the purpose of the Atlantic partnership on both sides of the Atlantic.

From the beginning, Atlantic cooperation was a requirement, as we all realize, for our security policy. Today, it is just as well, and in particular, a requirement for our economic policy.

Mr. President, you have come to our country at a very significant time. In a few days in Helsinki, the final phase of the Conference on Security and Cooperation in Europe will open. The negotiations in Geneva have set an example of the opportunities for constructive Western cooperation.

The negotiations have also shown—and your presence in Helsinki, Mr. President, will impressively demonstrate to the entire world—that America and Europe are inseparably linked, that one cannot talk about security and cooperation in Europe without including the United States. The Atlantic Alliance is part and parcel of Western Europe.

The Helsinki Conference should constitute another step towards détente. The documents to be signed provide a frame which needs to be filled in the future by agreements and concrete behavior. Each signatory state will then be able to demonstrate what it understands by détente.

This is the yardstick by which it will be measured. Nobody could wish more fervently than the Germans that the hopes tied to the Conference may be fulfilled.

Yet it is clear to us that no conference can guarantee our security. The Atlantic Alliance remains the foundation of our security.

Mr. President, you have already visited with your compatriots in the Federal Republic. The presence of the American soldiers in the Federal Republic and in Berlin is the clearest and the most important expression of the fact that the security of the United States and of Europe do belong together inseparably.

For the West, there is only one security. The Federal Republic contributes to the best of its ability to safeguard the common security. The American contribution, however, is irreplaceable and will remain so. Even a comprehensive European union, which is the goal of the member states of the European Community, cannot do without this transatlantic link.

We owe thanks to the American Government for having held fast to this policy unwaveringly. This is why over 400,000 American citizens live among us as soldiers, civilian employees, and families.

You can be sure, Mr. President, that we, citizens and authorities alike, do what we can to make your compatriots feel at home with us. They are our friends; they are our guests and the good comrades of the German soldiers.

Nevertheless, they do live in a different country with a different language and different customs, and over the long run that is not easy.

Therefore, permit me, Mr. President, to say to you, the highest representative of the American people, and to all Americans who are here in Germany for reasons of our common security, very simply and very warmly, thank you.

Mr. President, as you can see, we have many reasons to be glad about your visit. It makes us happy.

Once again, a cordial welcome to the white boat.

President Ford. President Scheel and distinguished guests:

Mr. President, you have spoken most generously and most farsightedly, as well as most eloquently, and I am pleased and honored to respond to such a gracious Rhinelander on this beautiful river, which has witnessed the growth of German-American cooperation.

I think there is something especially significant that an American President is on this wonderful river that includes from the headwaters in Switzerland, to France, to Germany, the Netherlands, and to the Atlantic.

There is something that seems to bind us all together, and I could not help but notice during the day, and as we have been sailing here tonight, many passing ships, some bearing flags of different nations, that this great river, as a result, symbolizes our hope for expanding the flow of peaceful commerce and the exchange throughout the world.

Just as many solid bridges span the majestic Rhine, strong links of friendship unite our two nations. I experienced today, Mr. President, this friendship anew when I met with Chancellor Schmidt and his associates, the distinguished leaders of your Government, and received the very warm welcome of so many citizens of your great country.

As we all know, our relationship is based upon a tradition that is as old as the United States itself, which now approaches its 200th year of freedom and democracy.

Every American schoolchild knows how General von Steuben came to help George Washington win the American Revolution. All

Americans are extremely proud of the infusion of German talents throughout the years into America, a nation of immigrants.

Today, I had the privilege, as you mentioned, to visit the military forces of our country and of yours, working in partnership, playing in partnership, and enjoying a family relationship in partnership.

It was an inspiring afternoon for me to meet the officers, the men on both sides, the German as well as the American. It is encouraging to me that they are working with a common zeal for a common purpose.

The commitment and the endeavor are very fundamental, as we know, to the security of the United States, to the Federal Republic and to Berlin, and to the entire Atlantic Alliance.

I thank you for the very, very warm welcome which the German people have extended to me, to Mrs. Ford, and to our son, Jack, but also to every American stationed here in the German Republic and their families.

Few people are more united than Americans and Germans in their support of the principles of independence, freedom, and self-determination.

Today, we speak of both the East as well as the West with new emphasis on a common future. Much effort has gone into increasing contacts and cooperation among the peoples of Europe. We have made some significant advances.

The forthcoming meeting, as you have mentioned, in Helsinki offers hope for future progress. Obviously, we have much further to go.

Americans do look forward to continued cooperation, not only with the Federal Republic but with the peoples of Europe as a whole.

Mr. President, a little more than a month has passed since we enjoyed you and Mrs. Scheel being in Washington and visiting us at the White House. The spirit prevailing among us today strongly reaffirms the genuine and continuing friendly relationship between our countries, our peoples, and our Government.

If you will raise your glass with me. I would like to propose a particularly cordial prosit to President Scheel and to the Federal Republic of Germany.

30

Speech by Chancellor Schmidt at Johns Hopkins University, July 16, 1976

On July 16, 1976, Chancellor Schmidt was awarded an honorary doctorate by Johns Hopkins University in Baltimore. In his remarks, Mr. Schmidt discussed historical and contemporary ties between Europe and the United States:

I am profoundly grateful for the high honor you are conferring upon me today. I am at the same time fully aware that I receive it as a stand-in, so to speak, for the spirit and the achievements of a democratic German state in the family of free and democratic nations in Europe. In other words, I am speaking to you today as witness to an achievement in which many participated and which could not have succeeded without the support of your country.

However much they may deserve it, not everyone can be honored in equal fashion—though, I might add, an old German dream would come true if everybody could address everybody else as "Herr Doktor" or even "Herr Professor."

According to all available information, members of the academic community are much more respected than humble politicians—at least in my country. I do not want to debate here and now whether such distrust of politicians is entirely justified—and in fact it may not even be justified with respect to all professors. Political figures—perhaps we can agree on that—may be more exposed in a moral sense, too. We have to live with that as best we can. Thus it is all the more comforting to note that, with this award, you are helping to foster reconciliation between the world of learning and the world of power, between the academies and the political arena; for in the history of my country—let me say this in all seriousness— these worlds during crucial periods of history have been tragically far apart. The gap often appeared unbridgeable. The founding of the United States, which you have been commemorating in so many festivities these past few weeks, relaxed and joyful and at the same time in rigorous self-examination, can be regarded as the most daring act of bridge-building between the world of learning and the realm of power ever attempted in the history of mankind.

It cannot be my role to debate before such a learned assembly the motives and the goals of the American revolution which have been interpreted a thousand times in recent months in a great internal dialogue here in your country.

124

It has, by the way, also been interpreted a thousand times this year in my own country.

But perhaps a European from Germany may be permitted to say a few words about the universal impact of the origins and rise of American democracy, for we Europeans too, sooner or later, were touched by the imprint of the great experiment which began 200 years ago and which has been described as the draft for a new society on a new earth.

It was indeed a "Grand Design" born, perhaps, of the hope for a "new man." If this was utopian, it was certainly not America's dream alone. Here in this country it has become, to use a fashionable American expression, a *concrete* utopia. But the *expectations* from which the experiment grew were as universal as its vision. Your historians have recorded that the spirit of enlightenment, which America was the first to transform into revolutionary action, reflected a kind of Atlantic unity.

Never before had similarly clear thought, similar purity of will, been allied with a similarly humane energy. The philosophers of England, the French encyclopedists, and Germany's Immanuel Kant, too, had long before thought about the right to life, to liberty, to individual freedom, but also to an ordinary wholesome life which Thomas Jefferson called "the pursuit of happiness."

During that age, the people of Europe sometimes seemed to have occasion—I am thinking of Frederick the Great of Prussia and others—to indulge in the illusion that their statesmen could be philosopher kings. That, to quote Henry Steele Commager, would have fulfilled Plato's dream that the world would be happy if it were ruled by philosophers.

But here—to quote once more Professor Commager—each and every town had its Solon and its Lykurg. No matter how modest the settlements of the colonists may have been in this continent, there always appear to have been some eminent citizens whose lives were oriented to an amazing degree to the precepts Europe had known since the days of ancient Greece and Rome.

Here, if anywhere at all, it was possible to fuse together the legacies of the Renaissance and the Reformation—the freedom in the worship of God which Luther had preached and the desire for a virtuous society which was part of the classical heritage; the hope for a "new Jerusalem," the "new Zion," "the city upon the hill"— the community in which Calvin's teachings were to find their earthly home—and the republican energies which were discussed by all educated citizens of this new world as America was built.

It was no accident that Gibbon's great study of the "Decline and Fall of the Roman Empire" was a bestseller in the year of the

125

American Revolution. And since I—having been taught by experience—do not underestimate economic conditions as a motive force of history, I might add that it cannot have been sheer coincidence that it was in 1776 that Adam Smith was to give the world the book that became the theoretical foundation of the era of economic liberalism—"The Wealth of Nations."

Whatever was thought, planned, desired in Europe, the founding fathers shared in the thoughts, the planning, the desires— and they translated them into reality. The sacred fires of which Jefferson said that they had to be guarded in America and to be carried forth into the world again and again, indeed quickly reached the old continent.

The French Revolution might perhaps have happened without the American Revolution—but there is no doubt that the American Revolution had a great intellectual impact upon the events in revolutionary France.

The French Declaration of Rights follows the Virginia Bill of Rights and the Declaration of Independence. However, revolutionary France translated the message of American liberties into a radicalism which appeared to touch the hearts of the people more profoundly. Cut off from religious roots, the utopian spirit also separated itself from the wholesome pragmatic adaptations of the American founding fathers.

It became an end in itself, without restraints, dissolving into the kind of abstraction that deteriorates into terror—into claiming the right to force upon man the happiness to which he is entitled, to impose upon society the welfare in which its destiny of freedom was to be fulfilled.

Then as now, freedom was endangered because people shunned the responsibilities that go along with it. Freedom needs confidence, responsibility, hope, determination in order to make individuality prevail within the system of dependencies that rule our existence. Freedom also needs a will for justice, not only in the legal but also the social sense of the word.

It remains true that, today, we are all children of a civilization that was strongly influenced by the American and the French Revolutions. It used to be said that each citizen of Europe had two fatherlands—his own and France. This reflects not only respect for the humanistic ideas that were articulated in 1789, but also the love of the cultural richness of every-day life in France; this is the deeper meaning behind the German saying: "Living like God in France." But the appreciation of this—which has come to me naturally in the past decades of close Franco-German partnership— needs to be enlarged upon.

To some degree—I feel—we have all become Americans. That is true for the Federal Republic of Germany which owes its existence in part to the understanding and foresight of what we might call a new elite of American "founding fathers"; it is true for the nations of Western Europe, for whose existence in freedom our Atlantic Alliance is a prerequisite.

But more than that. The reality of America has reached far beyond the circle of the classical democratic industrial nations, beyond the borders of the so-called Western world. It has been felt even where it is rejected; communist countries also are touched by its traces.

I was strangely moved upon reading that the Declaration of Independence of an Asian nation which had been enmeshed in a tragic conflict with America began with the words of Thomas Jefferson: "we hold these truths to be self-evident ... "

I do not overlook the fact that there are dangers inherent in this universal appeal. The missionary spirit sometimes appeared on the world stage rather impatiently and sometimes too innocently. It was already Jefferson who prophetically said "Old Europe will have to lean on our shoulders and to hobble along by our side" and exclaimed: "what a colossus shall we be ... a reliance for the reason and freedom of the globe."

Often enough nations resisted the demand to submit to this mission, and to this day the world is not "safe for democracy" as Woodrow Wilson, in an overexertion of good will, dreamed it would be.

It seems to me, America has learned from its darker experiences. It has in a mature manner abandoned the task of converting the world to its American ways.

The U.S. is no longer a world power against its will, and it is no longer impatient to settle all quarrels as the world's policeman. It has assumed its responsibility in the world in a more relaxed fashion.

I think the U.S. has freed itself from both the missionary and the isolationist motivations that are indeed so closely related to each other. It has got away from the extremes.

That is a crucial prerequisite for the system of partnership on which the world's equilibrium and hence peace does rest. If anywhere, the continuity of international politics must be sought here. There may be variants, nuances, minor shifts in priorities— but the structure of partnership remains our destiny.

I have no doubt that, as far as partnership is concerned, Americans and Europeans can fully rely on each other. Just as we cannot imagine life without a thousand signs of American civilization, so, too, is the uniting Western Europe inconceivable without the presence of the United States of America.

This presence is by no means limited to the stationing of troops. Nor am I talking only about the economic presence, which is important enough, but also about the political and intellectual presence which never threatens the independence or the "personality" of our European Community.

If Europe is to remain European there can be no anti-American Europe. That has even been understood by left-wing political forces on our continent. And it is no more possible for the United States to turn away from our old continent without jeopardizing its identity and its historic destiny. An America dissociated from Europe would cease to be the nation of Jefferson and Lincoln, Roosevelt, Eisenhower and Kennedy.

It is bitter enough to realize that we needed two world wars, their devastations and millions of dead, to accept the interdependence of our destinies. Now one can speak of indissoluble ties without risk of exaggeration; keen minds had envisioned this early in the day.

I have been told that Henry Adams—great grandson and grandson of American Presidents—while writing his memoirs in 1900, foresaw the choice Germany would have to make: It could either join a continental bloc, then it would be forced to seek the destruction of France and England; or it could find access to an "Atlantic system," as he called it, and the world would be spared decades of tensions and catastrophes.

Prophetic words, indeed. It seems to me, he went even further; he dreamed that one day Russia, too, might find entry into this "Atlantic system"—in perhaps 60 years. Counting from 1900, the world, he wrote, might have reached this apex of integration by the year 1960.

Reality has not caught up with Adams' vision, but a strange coincidence saw the policy of détente emerge at the beginning of the same decade. Its beginning was characterized by the Cuban missile crisis and President Kennedy's speech at the American University in Washington. It lived on in the conceptions of a Secretary of State to whom I do no injustice when I say that he brilliantly combined the legacy of the old world with the experience of the new world.

The elections of this year 1976 in America and in the Federal Republic of Germany—whatever their outcome—cannot destroy that continuity. This is going to be still further proof of the innate resilience of that policy.

Men of keen vision like Henry Adams prepared America for its responsibilities as a world power generations ago. I only wish that this America had been heard in the Kaiser's Germany, and that Adams had been understood at home. He perceived the contours of an alliance of industrialized nations, and he understood Europe's need for unification.

In contemplating his ideas it becomes remarkably clear that partnership with the United States is the Archimedian point from which alone the integration of Europe has become conceivable and possible.

This is no contradiction. There is, at this point, no rivalry or competition but only the realization that we depend on each other.

German-American relations cannot but gain from good relations between the United States and France, Great Britain and the other European partners. On the other hand, Germany's basic understanding with France, Great Britain and the others is an elementary condition for any European-American partnership worthy of this name.

And yet another indispensable point: the relations of the European nations among themselves and with America are determined by the quality of Franco-German friendship, by the growing symbiosis of our two peoples. Thus there is a certain logic in the fact that, corresponding to the process which has somewhat imprecisely been called the Americanization of Europe, there has been a cautious Europeanization of America.

My friend Willy Brandt recently raised the question—in Paris, significantly enough—whether one might speak today of a second Age of Enlightenment. Has the reluctant faith of earlier eras that there must be some universal reason become the compelling insight of today? I, too, would not dare answer that question.

But I find an affirmation in the mutual intellectual permeation of the old and the new world which, since the founding of America, has never been more intensive than it is today.

This has certainly been true of my country, about which one can say that only after World War II did it have a chance to translate the ideals of the democratic revolution into reality as they were developed by America and by France, and that Germany has only now succeeded in separating itself from its "apolitical culture."

It is only natural that my country, too—to return to what I said at the beginning—came closer to reconciling the world of the mind and the realm of power in this process—constructing the great bridge that was, and remains, the crucial goal of American independence.

We no longer understand politics as a total demand on human existence. Therefore we must no longer counter politics with an apolitical or antipolitical resistance stemming from the emotions, an attitude characterizing the conservative tradition in my country, so aptly described by Thomas Mann.

Rather have we finally accepted the morality of pragmatism of which Immanuel Kant spoke 200 years ago. That, too, is indeed a process of enlightenment—an enlightenment which goes far beyond naked rationalism, which reminds us that the word "enlightenment" implies more than simple devotion to reason, totally lacking a religious dimension.

The word speaks of "light." This hint, perhaps, explains the magic glow which surrounded the word "America" for many generations of Germans and their fellow Europeans. They were looking to this continent not only for prosperity, the big chance, quick riches, but for a new and different quality of life: the experience of liberty.

After the European catastrophes, this quality has finally found a home with us, too. We are grateful for that. The legacy of the hope that generations of emigrants carried with them to this country has returned to us.

Many of our fellow-countrymen, motivated by Europe's stubborn resistance to the experiment of freedom and justice, have helped shape the political and intellectual foundations of the United States—the farmers and ministers whom William Penn called to America, the refugees of 1848 who conceived of the ideal state as a republic of scholars, the emigrants who could not have saved their very lives but for America's protection against Nazi tyranny and violence.

It has been said that the Germans in this country have become such good Americans that they are no longer recognizable as Germans. That is only a half-truth it seems to me, but it is not a bad testimony, neither to America nor to its Germans.

In some fortunate cases there has been a particularly fruitful blending of elements, in this city of Baltimore more noticeably then elsewhere, and never more excitingly than in the figure of H. L. Mencken, who might perhaps be called a happy Voltaire for America of this century and for the man in the street.

I was a little shocked when I found in one of his writings the claim that the Germans, "delivered from the Hohenzollerns, now find the Schmidts and the Krauses ten times as expensive and oppressive." But I was even more amused by the exaggerations of this satirist. Only an archrepublican can mock the republic, only a committed democrat can mock democracy that coolly.

Life, undoubtedly, has become more expensive. But since then the Schmidts have gained something of a reputation for fighting inflation. And German chancellors in the center of Europe before Germany turned to pragmatic reason, which combines the best of its own heritage, of European examples, and of American development.

I do not think I have done any injustice to the spirit of this location by quoting him only at my own expense. H. L. Mencken fearlessly pleaded in one of his essays for a "Realpolitik" which he translated literally as "realism in politics." Interpreted in this way, one may welcome this much abused word.

Realism in politics appears to me the only guarantee of the preservation of a reasonable system which does keep the world in balance or equilibrium.

Realism necessarily means a policy of peace. Realism means equilibrium. Realism means a policy of social justice preparing the way for general welfare and the pursuit of happiness. Realism finally means recognizing the limits of our means and recognizing the limits of our power.

Thus one may understand Realpolitik as a call for moderation. To me this moderation is a crucial element of the "New Enlightenment" which is becoming the test of our age. Only moderation offers a chance to solve the problems of our time. Only the spread of reason can guarantee our survival.

But that is only another way of saying what was recently said at a political convention in this country: "The American idea ... is realized in each of us."

These words, spoken by a black U.S. citizen, confirm the universal message of the American Revolution. That message has had an impact on us, too. We have not forgotten that we are Germans, Frenchmen, Englishmen, or Italians. But thanks to America, our existence has become more human. I know of no better way of describing our spirit of neighborhood and partnership.

Thank you.

31

Remarks by Chancellor Schmidt
July 13, 1977, on the Occasion of his
Meeting With President Carter

Chancellor Schmidt and President Carter conversing at the White House, Washington, during the Chancellor's visit to the United States July 13–14, 1977.

During his visit to Washington, Chancellor Schmidt responded as follows to a dinner speech by President Carter:

The Chancellor. Mr. President, Mrs. Carter,
ladies and gentlemen:

Let me say first that I as a person am deeply moved by the generous words you just said. And I would like to express my personal gratitude, but express my thanks also on behalf of Minister Genscher and all our delegation. I would ask your permission to use a few notes which I have drafted this afternoon, being on a little handicap with your language.

And I would like to say that we today have carried on from where we left it off in London in May. Our meetings were preceded by Vice President Mondale's visit to my country. It's sad that he had to go back to the Senate tonight and didn't get a supper.

The President.

He's come back.

The Chancellor.

Has he come back? You are wandering between the two places. [*Laughter*] But coming from a parliamentary democracy, and having been a Member of Parliament myself for 24 years, I know how it is. [*Laughter*]

This picture of close and sincere and trustful consultations between ourselves has been rounded off by various personal contacts between our foreign ministers and also by telephone and written communications between ourselves. The intensity of our dialog, to me, is a reflection of the unprecedented state of relations between the United States and the Federal Republic of Germany. It's a reflection also of the depth of our common, basic beliefs and basic convictions, a reflection also of our common interests and of the fact that the friendly nature of our meetings is very much a matter of course.

It's on this solid foundation of human and political links that this present meeting is based, like others in the past and more to come in the future.

I would like to emphasize already now that the talks and discussions of this first day of our stay in Washington, D.C., have been very fruitful and constructive.

I once again was deeply impressed by the profound sense of responsibility and understanding which you showed, Mr. President, when we were dealing with important aspects of international politics. And I once more have become aware of the tremendous burden which the President of the United States has to carry. His decisions very often have repercussions, consequences far beyond the borders of the United States. He needs great strength. His office requires confidence, and it does ask for an open mind with regards to the numerous problems which challenge the leading Western power.

Let me add that I have great admiration for the way in which President Carter is performing his tasks, and I would like to add for you personally, Jimmy, the way you have welcomed us today, to me, is just another proof of the common ground on which we stand, not only on general terms but also as friends working closely together.

We all know that the manifold problems facing the world today call more than ever for common effort and that they can be solved only if we proceed on the basis of common responsibility.

The Federal Republic of Germany will render its full contribution. And you, Mr. President, and your fellow Americans can rely on our firm will to pursue our common goals in close cooperation with you.

And I am quite sure that I can say this for all the citizens in my country, for all the German nation, as much as I can say this for all the members of my delegation, which as you already mentioned does not only consist of political leaders and civil servants but also eminent leaders from the trade unions, from industry, and from our cultural life and from our mass media.

We all know that the strength, quite a bit of the strength, and the confidence which you projected into our nation a couple of minutes ago—that they derive from the knowledge that my people can face up to great challenges of our times side by side with the United States.

I am convinced that our visit will help to even further increase, as you said, the determination and energy with which we on both sides of the Atlantic set about our great tasks.

We share with you, Mr. President, and with your country, and with your nation, the belief in the superiority of the spirit of freedom of the individual person. And like you, we are convinced that freedom can only prevail if the dignity of the individual and his or her civil rights, or as they are being called in our constitution, basic rights, are respected and exercised.

At the same time, we German people know from a bitter epoch in our history that freedom and basic rights can never be taken for granted, that they only thrive when they are protected and preserved by sincerity, by courageous involvement, and even by sacrifice.

You will always find the Federal Republic of Germany and its people at your side when it comes to safeguarding freedom for the individual and securing respect for his or her dignity and rights around the world.

I guess we need no special capacity of perception to recognize that without the Atlantic Alliance, which is the visible expression of our harmony in these objectives, freedom and basic rights in the western part of Europe might have been imperiled, perhaps even extinguished, in some parts over the past three decades.

We Germans never regarded the presence of the United States in Europe as part of a power political calculation, but we always regarded it an involvement stemming from a deep commitment, for which we are grateful and which we reciprocate for the very same reason.

It becomes equally clear against this background how much importance is being attached to the patient continuance of the policy of détente, starting from the safe basis of our alliance and of its ability to defend ourselves.

Let me stress in this context that it is the most vital interest of my divided nation to continue and to further this policy of alleviating tensions, because there just is no other way to try and alleviate the human problems in millions of families in my nation stemming from the political and geographical division of my people.

There is, of course, a strong connection between elimination or alleviation of tensions in Europe and in other parts of the world and in the realization of all the three baskets of the Helsinki declaration, as was stressed by Secretary Vance just a couple of days ago.

One glance at the map or at the geopolitical and military facts shows ourselves the enormous differences between our two countries—at least some of the enormous differences between our two countries. In the United States people might not always realize that my country is no larger than the State of Oregon, with the one exception that there are living more than 60 million in that little state of the Federal Republic of Germany, 60 or 62 million.

Of course, no offense is being meant—no offense toward the good citizens of the State of Oregon—[laughter]—is being meant in using their fine State as a yardstick for the smallness in territory of my home country. I'm very well aware of the importance of Oregon, and of Portland especially. [Laughter]

But I like to point to the smallness of my country in order to make it understood that neither are we a world power nor do we want to become one. We see ourselves as a European country integrating itself within the European community, with responsibilities determined by its membership in that community, responsibilities by its membership within the North Atlantic Alliance, responsibilities by our role in the economic system of the world. And we see our role as a country with very, very limited natural resources only.

To my view and to the view of most of my countrymen, intra-European cooperation and the Atlantic Alliance complement each other. And for us Germans, both of them are indispensable. Therefore, I welcome the practice of your administration to conduct particularly intensive consultations with European allies, with ourselves, and I have the feeling that our meeting today proves that this is not just theory but a very practical and successful reality.

My wife and I and the members of my delegation are grateful for your hospitality, Mr. President, which you have extended to us here in Washington. We are really glad of the opportunity to discuss questions and problems with close friends here in the United States in, as you correctly say, a frank and openhearted manner, even if there may arise some points on which we might differ.

I do feel that if the world could show many more examples of talks conducted in such a spirit, the world would be quite a different and much better place.

I would now like to ask my fellow countrymen to raise their glasses and drink with me to the health of the President of the United States, Jimmy Carter, to continuing happiness of the American people, and to ever closer cooperation and friendship between our two nations.

32

Speech by President Carter During His Visit to Bonn, July 14, 1978

President Carter made the following speech at a state dinner while on an official visit to the Federal Republic of Germany July 13–15, 1978:

Mr. President, Chancellor Schmidt, distinguished members of the government, economic society of the Federal Republic of Germany, ladies and gentlemen, my friends:

We who have come from Washington to visit your great country know that we are among friends. I want to express my deep appreciation for the generous reception that all of you have given to us and to offer my thanks to the citizens of the Federal Republic of Germany who have greeted us so warmly.

It's a pleasure to begin my first visit to the Federal Republic as President in the city that nurtured Beethoven—a symbol not only of German culture but also of the indomitable spirit of a free people. There are two great musicians that I have admired in Germany—Ludwig van Beethoven and President Scheel. [*Laughter*]

But Bonn is equally significant in the contemporary role as the capital of this great and vibrant nation. The political and economic development of Western Europe since World War II is one of the greatest success stories in modern history. Mass poverty has been replaced by mass prosperity. Century-old enemies have become political allies and are together building the future of Europe.

And here in Germany you have established and maintained a strong and a stable democracy. As the capital of West Germany, Bonn symbolizes the will and the determination of free people. You are a model in a livable world—a world we can manage, a world we can afford, a world we can enjoy.

Here in this peaceful young capital in the shadow of Siebengebirge, it is possible to envision a day when all nations will have revitalized cities surrounded by rural plenty, a day when all nations will cherish freedom, will understand the function of dissent in a free society, and offer their citizens the right to share in making the decisions that affect their own lives.

As I drove through Bonn today, I saw superbly restored old buildings standing proudly beside splendid new structures. I think this growing capital city that you enjoy is as strong a testimony to the vitality of modern Germany as your remarkable deutschemark.

The United States is very proud of its long and intimate association with West Germany. We have watched with admiration—sometimes with envy—as you became one of the outstanding economies and the outstanding trading countries of the entire world.

For the last two decades, your economy has provided a powerful stimulus for the growth in Europe. Your policies are consistently among the most constructive on the Continent, indeed, the entire world. And you play an essential role in the developing economic strength of the global economy. They are even more impressive—your policies are—in the context of your commitment to a free market system and the ideals of a free society.

That commitment is even more significant at a time when terrorist groups wrongly believe that they can force free societies to abandon our liberties. Our two nations are steadfast in our resolve to end the menace of terrorism and in our resolute conviction that democratic liberty and social justice are the best answers to terrorist threats. The application of civil protections in your exemplary basic law is ample evidence of the Federal Republic's devotion to these libertarian ideals.

The affinity between the Federal Republic and the United States goes well beyond our own bilateral interests, even well beyond those of the Atlantic community.

Our nations understand the moral force of democracy. This is the fundamental strength of the German-American partnership. Our peoples understand the meaning of fair access to opportunity and just reward. These shared convictions help us to face our problems in a spirit of cooperation. They give us the tools and the confidence to meet the challenges, difficult challenges of a modern society.

Our agenda—and the agenda for all democracies—includes a renewed commitment to global economic well-being. This, more than any other material goal, promises a future in keeping with the age-old yearnings of mankind: an end to inequities among nations, as well as among classes of citizens; a day when an interdependent world of trade and commerce can generate an adequate number of jobs, better income, and a better life in the poor two-thirds of the world; a day when the continuing transfer of capital and technology from rich to poorer countries will have spread the benefits of the industrialized nations throughout the underdeveloped world.

This transfer of funds and services is just as important to our own economic health as it is to the well-being of the less-developed countries. In 2 days, Chancellor Schmidt and I will sit down with our colleagues from the United Kingdom, France, Canada, Italy,

Japan, and the European Commission to develop strategies to achieve the goals which I have just outlined. This will be the fourth economic summit conference and I approach it with optimism.

Although we have not achieved all we had hoped in the 14 months since the last summit conference in London, I share the feelings that were expressed there in a very heartfelt way by Prime Minister Fukuda. When we met at Downing Street last year, he reminded us that the Great Depression, even the war in the Pacific, might have been prevented if world leaders had met again after the breakdown of the London Economic Conference in 1930, and suggested that while we may not achieve all we hope for, we may prevent more than we realize.

Let me say, first, that we meet acutely aware that currency fluctuations, labor migrations, crop failures, and a host of other variables respect no political or geographical boundary; that every event that once was isolated affects each aspect of today's integrated global economy. We are mutually vulnerable to and totally and equally dependent upon each other.

Together we must seek stable, noninflationary growth and jobs for our people.

Together we must seek to expand and to liberalize international trade policies and to put an end to rising protectionist sentiment.

Together we must seek a multilateral trade agreement that enhances and not obstructs world commerce.

Together we must seek to reduce energy consumption and to encourage energy exploration and production.

Together we must seek an international monetary system strong enough and flexible enough to sustain growth and to bolster confidence.

Together we must seek to share the benefits of economic progress and expanded trade with all the developing nations and channel increased aid to the world's neediest countries.

The United States and the Federal Republic are united in our commitment to these objectives. More is at stake than our economic well-being. Economic strength gives us the means and the confidence and spirit to deter war and to ensure peace.

What we do here in Bonn this week, and at home in the weeks ahead, relates directly to our military as well as our economic security.

Our defense policy is based on a strong NATO. American security is tied as closely to the security of Western Europe today as it has been for the past three decades. We are prepared to deter war in Europe and to defend all allied territory, as strongly and as deeply committed as we defend the territory of the United States itself.

Tomorrow I will visit a few of the 200,000 American NATO troops stationed in Germany and the German troops who serve with them. I will assure them of this continuing commitment of the people whom I represent.

When the NATO summit met in Washington 6 weeks ago, we agreed on a Long-Term Defense Program, 15 years, that will guarantee the men the supplies and the equipment to meet any foreseeable military threat. This was not a unilateral commitment; it was a pledge made by the Alliance itself. All the Allies agreed to increase our military budget; all of us agreed to share the responsibilities of our long term security.

The work we do together in strengthening the global economy and providing for our mutual security gives us the confidence that we seek to reduce tension with our potential adversaries.

We realize that our relationship with the Soviet Union will continue to be competitive for a long time to come and that the Soviets will continue to pose threats and challenges to Western interests. But we also recognize the threat to peace posed by a continuation of the arms race or by our inability to move beyond confrontation.

We are prepared to broaden our areas of cooperation with the Soviet Union, to seek a genuine, broadly defined, and fully reciprocal détente. We hope the Soviets will choose to join with us in making this effort. For our part we intend to make clear that we continue to seek cooperation, but we are fully prepared to protect Western interests.

Today the United States is negotiating a SALT II agreement that will preserve and enhance our own security and that of our Allies, indeed, the entire world. Reaching that agreement is essential to meeting the broad responsibilities shared by the Soviet Union and the United States to nations and to people everywhere.

We are prepared to negotiate in other areas—to seek reductions in the level of conventional forces in Europe, to limit nuclear testing, and to put a halt to further proliferation of nuclear explosives.

But genuine détente also includes restraint in the use of military power and an end to the pursuit of unilateral advantage— as in Africa today. And détente must include the honoring of solemn international agreements concerning human rights and a mutual effort to promote a climate in which these rights can flourish.

If the Soviet Union chooses to join in developing a more broad-based and reciprocal détente, the world will reap untold benefits. But whatever the Soviets decide, the West will do whatever is necessary to preserve our security while we continue, without ceasing, the search for a lasting peace. We will maintain our own strength as a clear indication of our commitment to free, democratic institutions, and our continuing obligation to our NATO Allies.

In my very short time in the Federal Republic of Germany, I have gained a deeper sense of the fundamental strength and the mutual benefit to be derived from our partnership. I believe that we will achieve the peaceful and the prosperous world we seek together.

I hope that you will join me now in a toast: To world peace and to the close and enduring German-American friendship and to the health of President Scheel.

To peace, and to your health, Mr. President. Thank you very much. Thank you, everybody.

33

Statements by President Reagan and Chancellor Schmidt at Their Meeting on May 21, 1981

Chancellor Schmidt taking leave of President Reagan on the White House lawn, Washington, May 22, 1981.

On May 21, 1981, in Washington, Chancellor Schmidt met for the first time with newly-elected President Ronald Reagan. At the welcoming ceremony both statesmen spoke of their planned consultations within the framework of a long history of relations between the two countries and peoples:

The President.

Chancellor Schmidt, one of the warmest greetings that Americans can offer in welcoming a guest into their midst is to say, "Make yourself at home." On behalf of our fellow citizens, Nancy and I hope that you and Mrs. Schmidt will make yourselves at home during your visit to the United States. We remember with great pleasure how welcome and at home you made us feel on our visit to Germany in 1978.

As you know, millions of German immigrants over the years have made America their home. With strong hands and good hearts, these industrious people helped build a strong and good America. But as proud as they were of this country, they didn't forget their German heritage. They named towns in the New World after those in the Old. The Federal Republic of Germany has just one Bremen: the Federal Republic has one, but we have Bremens in Indiana, in Georgia, and Ohio. And our States are dotted with Hamburgs and Berlins. In honor of Baron von Steuben, the Prussian officer who aided our revolution, we have cities and towns in a number of States named after him. But I hope you'll forgive us, over the years we've sort of anglicized the pronunciation. We call them now Steubens and Steubenvilles. And the list goes on from Heidelberg, Mississippi, to Stuttgart, Arkansas.

But the Federal Republic of Germany and the United States of America share more than a common background and a well-established friendship. We share values about the importance of liberty. This year marks the 20th anniversary of the Berlin Wall, a border of brutality that assaults the human spirit and the civilized mind. On one side of the wall, people live in dignity and democracy; on the other side, in domination and defeat. We of the United States are aware of this relentless pressure on the Federal Republic and her citizens, and we admire you for your courage in the face of such grim realities.

The Federal Republic is perched on the cliff of freedom that overlooks Soviet dependents to the East. While the dominated peoples in these lands cannot enjoy your liberties, they can look at your example and hope. The United States is proud to stand beside you as your beacon shines brightly from that cliff of freedom.

We both recognize the challenges posed to our security by those who do not share our beliefs and our objectives. And together, we will act to counter those dangers. The United States will work in partnership with you and with our other European allies to bolster NATO and to offset the disturbing buildup of Soviet military forces. At the same time, we will work toward meaningful negotiations to limit those very weapons.

Mr. Chancellor, under your thoughtful and responsible leadership, the Federal Republic has sought to ease tensions in a world taut and quivering with the strains of instability—not only between East and West but between North and South. And we're aware of the Federal Republic's other contributions as well. Americans remember that when the United States sought support in freeing

American prisoners in Iran, the Federal Republic stood firmly by us and we thank you for that support.

Although the Federal Republic, like the United States, is not immune to economic difficulties, the Communist countries cannot help but compare your well-being to their own shortages and hardships.

Our economic policies should be as closely allied as our defense policies, for in the end, our military capabilities are dependent on the strengths of our economies. Sound fiscal management was the hallmark of the Federal Republic's economic miracle, and we in the United States intend to import some of that responsibility to gain control of our own economy.

Chancellor Schmidt, I began these remarks speaking of German immigrants who came to America. Let me mention one immigrant in particular—Johann Augustus Roebling, the man who built the Brooklyn Bridge, which at its opening in 1883 was called the eighth wonder of the world. Well, Mr. Roebling spanned more than the East River with his accomplishment; he spanned two countries and two peoples. The discussions we have today will span our common goals and bridge our joint concerns. They will set the scene for the closest possible consultations in the future.

We have come to rely on one another in times of calm and in times of crisis, and that certainly is the basis of a true friend-partnership. It is in that spirit that I look forward to the important talks ahead.

And again, *"Herzlich Willkommen* [a hearty welcome]."

The Chancellor. Mr. President, Mrs. Reagan, ladies and gentlemen:

Thank you very much, Mr. President, for your cordial reception and your most friendly words of welcome.

This is not the first time I've been here, but on each occasion I'm impressed by the authority and dignity which radiates from this seat of Government of the mighty United States of America. I am very glad to have this opportunity for an exchange of views with you, Mr. President, on major issues which both of us have much on our minds.

I cannot tell you how happy I am to know that you have recovered so well from the treacherous attempt on your life on the 30th of March. We in Germany have followed your rapid progress with much feeling, sir, and with a great sense of relief.

My visit to Washington is taking place against the background of a serious international situation. At the beginning of the Eighties, we are confronted with a whole range of problems and challenges. I need only mention the excessive Soviet arms build-up, the challenge toward the community of nations resulting from the continuing Soviet intervention in Afghanistan, the threat to the non-alignment of the Third World countries stemming from unresolved political conflicts and as a result of East-West conflicts being transferred to their part of the world. And I need only mention, also, the impact of the oil price explosion on the whole world economy.

The Western democracies will be able to cope with these challenges if they show their determination, if they do take joint action, and if they let themselves be guided by the principles of consistency, predictability, and reliability.

Three weeks ago in Rome, Italy, our Alliance gave a clear signal for the continuity of our common policies. I regarded this as a proof of the Alliance's political strength. And as I said in the German Parliament 2 weeks ago, I also regard it as a success for your new administration, sir, here in Washington, D.C.

German-American partnership is today again manifest in the wide-ranging consultations between you, Mr. President, and the German head of Government. Good and reliable relations between the Federal Republic of Germany and the United States of America are, in my view, a major factor for the security of the West and for international stability. I am confident that this visit will help us to fulfill our common responsibilities.

Thank you very much.

34

Joint Statement of May 22, 1981, on the Occasion of Chancellor Schmidt's Visit

The following joint statement was issued by both parties at the conclusion of their discussions:

During the official visit of Chancellor Helmut Schmidt of the Federal Republic of Germany to the United States from May 20–23, 1981, President Reagan and the Federal Chancellor held detailed talks on a wide range of political and economic questions. They noted with satisfaction that they share a common assessment of the international situation and its implications for the Western Alliance. They agreed that their two countries have a common destiny founded on joint security interests and firmly rooted in their shared values of liberty, a democratic way of life, self-determination and belief in the inalienable rights of man.

They regard the reliable and proven U.S.-German partnership as an essential factor in international stability and Western security based on the North Atlantic Alliance. They agreed that substantive and effective consultations are a mainstay of the relations between Western Europe and the United States.

The President the the Federal Chancellor welcomed and reaffirmed the results of the recent NATO Ministerial meetings in Rome and Brussels as renewed proof of the political strength of the Alliance and the continuity of Alliance policy. They stressed the determination of Alliance members to take the necessary steps to work with their NATO partners to strengthen the Western defense posture and to address adverse trends due to the Soviet military buildup. Together with deterrence and defense, arms control and disarmament are integral parts of Alliance security policy.

The President and the Federal Chancellor affirmed in this connection their resolve to implement both elements of the NATO decision of December 1979 and to give equal weight to both elements. The Federal Chancellor welcomed the U.S. decision to begin negotiations with the Soviet Union on the limitation of theater nuclear weapons within the SALT framework by the end of this year. He also welcomed the fact that the U.S. Secretary of State has initiated preparatory discussions on theater nuclear forces with the Soviet Union, looking toward an agreement to begin formal negotiations. The President and the Federal Chancellor agreed that TNF modernization is essential for Alliance security and as a basis for parallel negotiations leading to concrete results on limitations of theater nuclear forces. They further agreed that the preparatory studies called for in the Rome Communique should be undertaken as matters of immediate priority by the relevant NATO bodies.

The President and the Federal Chancellor assessed very favorably the close cooperation between the Federal Republic of Germany and the Three Powers in matters relating to Berlin and Germany as a whole. The Federal Chancellor thanked the President for his reaffirmation of the pledge that the United States will continue to guarantee the security and viability of Berlin. They agreed that the maintenance of the calm situation in and around Berlin is of crucial significance for European security and stability.

The European Community plays an important part in maintaining international political and economic stability. The U.S. will continue to support the process of European unification.

Both sides noted that a serious international situation has been created by Soviet expansionism and armaments efforts. To meet this challenge and to secure peace, they are determined to respond with firmness and to maintain a dialogue with the Soviet Union.

The President and the Federal Chancellor agreed that it is important for the stabilization of East-West relations that the current CSCE Review Conference in Madrid agree on a balanced substantive concluding document which includes enhanced respect for human rights, increased human contracts, a freer flow of information, and cooperation among and security for all of the participants. In this regard, and as part of such a balanced result, the President and the Chancellor favor agreement on a precise mandate for a conference on disarmament in Europe, providing for the application of militarily significant, binding and verifiable confidence-building measures covering all of the continent of Europe from the Atlantic to the Urals.

Poland must be allowed to solve its problems peacefully and without external interference. The President and the Federal Chancellor reaffirmed unequivocally their view that any external intervention would have the gravest consequences for international relations and would fundamentally change the entire international situation.

Genuine nonalignment of the states of the developing world is an important stabilizing factor in international relations. The Chancellor and the President support the independence and the right of self-determination of the states of the developing world. They will, in concert with their Allies and the countries affected, oppose any attempts, direct or indirect, by the Soviet Union to undermine the independence and stability of these states. They confirmed their willingness to continue their cooperation with these states on the basis of equal partnership and to continue their support of their economic development.

The President and the Federal Chancellor reaffirmed their view that the Soviet occupation of Afghanistan is unacceptable. They demanded the withdrawal of Soviet troops from Afghanistan and respect for that country's right to return to independence and nonalignment. The destabilizing effects which the Soviet intervention in Afghanistan has on the entire region must be countered.

Both sides stressed the importance of broad-based cooperation with the states of the Gulf Region.

The President and the Federal Chancellor agreed that the United States and the Federal Republic of Germany, the latter within the framework of European political cooperation, should continue the search for a comprehensive, just and lasting peace in the Middle East. Their efforts should continue to be complementary and build upon what has been achieved so far.

Both sides reaffirmed the determination to strengthen further the open system of world trade and to oppose pressure for protectionist measures.

They stressed the vital importance for political and economic stability of further energy conservation and diversification measures to reduce the high degree of dependence on oil. The pressing energy problems can only be mastered on the basis of world-wide cooperative efforts that strengthen Western energy security and reduce the vulnerability of the West to potential supply cutoffs from any source. The supply problems of the developing countries require particular attention.

The President and the Federal Chancellor agreed on the need in framing their economic policies to give high priority to the fight against inflation and to the creation of improved conditions for renewed economic growth and increased productivity. Both sides stressed the need for a close coordination of economic policies among the industrial countries.

Both sides stressed the need for close and comprehensive exchange of views on the United Nations Conference on the Law of the Sea while the U.S. Government reviews its position.

The President and the Federal Chancellor noted that their talks once more demonstrated the friendly and trusting relationship that has linked their two countries for over 30 years. They welcomed all efforts which serve to broaden mutual contacts and underlined the responsibility of the coming generation for maintaining and developing German-American friendship.

148

35

Address by President Reagan Before the Bundestag in Bonn, June 9, 1982

President Reagan addressing the Bundestag, Bonn, June 9, 1982. Behind President Reagan: Bundestag President Richard Stücklen.

In a speech before the West German Parliament during a visit to the Federal Republic of Germany June 9–11 President Reagan outlined his ideas on questions of security and arms control:

I am very honored to speak to you today and thus to all the people of Germany. Next year we will jointly celebrate the 300th anniversary of the first German settlement in the American colonies. The 13 families who came to our new land were the forerunners of more than 7 million German immigrants to the United States. Today more Americans claim German ancestry than any other.

These Germans cleared and cultivated our land, built our industries, and advanced our arts and sciences. In honor of 300 years of German contributions in America, President Carstens and I have agreed today that he will pay an official visit to the United States in October of 1983 to celebrate the occasion.

The German people have given us so much; we like to think that we've repaid some of that debt. Our American Revolution was the first revolution in modern history to be fought for the right of self-government and the guarantee of civil liberties. That spirit was contagious. In 1849 the Frankfurt Parliament's statement of basic human rights guaranteed freedom of expression, freedom of religion, and equality before the law. These principles live today in the basic law of the Federal Republic. Many peoples to the east still wait for such rights.

The United States is proud of your democracy, but we cannot take credit for it. Heinrich Heine, in speaking of those who built the awe-inspiring cathedrals of medieval times, said that "in those days people had convictions. We moderns have only opinions and it requires something more than opinions to build a Gothic cathedral." Over the past 30 years, the convictions of the German people have built a cathedral of democracy—a great and glorious testament to your ideals.

We in America genuinely admire the free society you have built in only a few decades. And we understand all the better what you have accomplished because of our own history. Americans speak with the deepest reverence of those founding fathers and first citizens who gave us the freedoms we enjoy today. And even though they lived over 200 years ago, we carry them in our hearts as well as our history books.

I believe future generations of Germans will look to you here today and to your fellow Germans with the same profound respect and appreciation. You have built a free society with an abiding faith in human dignity—the crowning ideal of Western civilization. This will not be forgotten. You will be saluted and honored by this republic's descendants over the centuries to come.

Yesterday, before the British Parliament, I spoke of the values of Western civilization and the necessity to help all peoples gain the institutions of freedom. In many ways, in many places, our ideals are being tested today. We are meeting this afternoon between two important summits, the gathering of leading industrial democracies at Versailles and the assembling of the Atlantic alliance here in Bonn tomorrow. Critical and complex problems face us. But our dilemmas will be made easier if we remember our partnership is based on a common Western heritage and a faith in democracy.

The Search For Peace

I believe this partnership of the Atlantic alliance nations is motivated primarily by the search for peace. Inner peace for our citizens and peace among nations. Why inner peace? Because democracy

150

allows for self-expression. It respects man's dignity and creativity. It operates by rule of law, not by terror or coercion. It is government with the consent of the governed. As a result, citizens of the Atlantic alliance enjoy an unprecedented level of material and spiritual well-being. And they are free to find their own personal peace.

We also seek peace among nations. The psalmist said: "Seek peace and pursue it." Our foreign policies are based on this principle and directed toward this end. The noblest objective of our diplomacy is the patient and difficult task of reconciling our adversaries to peace. And I know we all look forward to the day when the only industry of war will be the research of historians.

But the simple hope for peace is not enough. We must remember something Friedrich Schiller said, "The most pious man can't stay in peace if it doesn't please his evil neighbor." So there must be a method to our search, a method that recognizes the dangers and realities of the world. During Chancellor Schmidt's state visit to Washington last year, I said that your republic was "perched on a cliff of freedom." I wasn't saying anything the German people do not already know. Living as you do in the heart of a divided Europe, you can see more clearly than others that there are governments at peace neither with their own peoples nor the world.

I don't believe any reasonable observer can deny there is a threat to both peace and freedom today. It is as stark as a gash of a border that separates the German people. We are menaced by a power that openly condemns our values and answers our restraint with a relentless military buildup.

We cannot simply assume every nation wants the peace we so earnestly desire. The Polish people would tell us there are those who would use military force to repress others who want only basic human rights. The freedom fighters of Afghanistan would tell us as well that the threat of aggression has not receded from the world.

Strengthening Alliance Security

Without a strengthened Atlantic security, the possibility of military coercion will be very great. We must continue to improve our defenses if we are to preserve peace and freedom. This is not an impossible task; for almost 40 years, we have succeeded in deterring war. Our method has been to organize our defensive capabilities, both nuclear and conventional, so that an aggressor could have no hope of military victory. The alliance has carried its strength not as a battle flag but as a banner of peace. Deterrence has kept that peace, and we must continue to take the steps necessary to make deterrence credible.

151

This depends in part on a strong America. A national effort, entailing sacrifices by the American people, is now underway to make long-overdue improvements in our military posture. The American people support this effort because they understand how fundamental it is to keeping the peace they so fervently desire.

We also are resolved to maintain the presence of well-equipped and trained forces in Europe, and our strategic forces will be modernized and remain committed to the alliance. By these actions, the people of the United States are saying, "We are with you Germany. You are not alone." Our adversaries would be foolishly mistaken should they gamble that Americans would abandon their alliance responsibilities, no matter how severe the test.

Alliance security depends on a fully credible conventional defense to which all allies contribute. There is a danger that any conflict would escalate to a nuclear war. Strong conventional forces can make the danger of conventional or nuclear conflict more remote. Reasonable strength in and of itself is not bad; it is honorable when used to maintain peace or defend deeply held beliefs.

One of the first chores is to fulfill our commitments to each other by continuing to strengthen our conventional defenses. This must include improving the readiness of our standing forces and the ability of those forces to operate as one. We must also apply the West's technological genius to improving our conventional deterrence.

There can be no doubt that we as an alliance have the means to improve our conventional defenses. Our peoples hold values of individual liberty and dignity that time and again they have proven willing to defend. Our economic energy vastly exceeds that of our adversaries. Our free system has produced technological advantages that other systems, with their stifling ideologies, cannot hope to equal. All of these resources are available to our defense.

Yes, many of our nations currently are experiencing economic difficulties. Yet we must nevertheless guarantee that our security does not suffer as a result. We've made strides in conventional defense over the last few years despite our economic problems, and we have disproved the pessimists who contend that our efforts are futile. The more we close the conventional gap, the less the risks of aggression or nuclear conflict.

The soil of Germany, and every other ally, is of vital concern to each member of the alliance, and this fundamental commitment is embodied in the North Atlantic Treaty. But it will be an empty pledge unless we insure that American forces are ready to reinforce Europe and Europe is ready to receive them. I am encouraged by the recent agreement on wartime host-nation support. This pact strengthens our ability to deter aggression in Europe and demonstrates our common determination to respond to attack.

Just as each ally shares fully in the security of the alliance, each is responsible for shouldering a fair share of the burden. Now that, of course, often leads to a difference of opinion, and criticism of our alliance is as old as the partnership itself.

But voices have been raised on both sides of the Atlantic that mistake the inevitable process of adjustment within the alliance for a dramatic divergence of interests. Some Americans think that Europeans are too little concerned for their own security; some would unilaterally reduce the number of American troops deployed in Europe. And in Europe itself, we hear the idea that the American presence, rather than contributing to peace, either has no deterrent value or actually increases the risk that our allies may be attacked.

These arguments ignore both the history and the reality of the trans-Atlantic coalition. Let me assure you that the American commitment to Europe remains steady and strong. Europe's shores are our shores. Europe's borders are our borders. And we will stand with you in defense of our heritage of liberty and dignity. The American people recognize Europe's substantial contributions to our joint security. Nowhere is that contribution more evident than here in the Federal Republic. German citizens host the forces of six nations. German soldiers and reservists provide the backbone of NATO's conventional deterrent in the heartland of Europe. Your *Bundeswehr* is a model for the integration of defense needs with a democratic way of life. And you have not shrunk from the heavy responsibility of accepting the nuclear forces necessary for deterrence.

I ask your help in fulfilling another responsibility. Many American citizens don't believe that their counterparts in Europe—especially younger citizens—really understand the U.S. presence there. If you will work toward explaining the U.S. role to people on this side of the Atlantic, I will explain it to those on the other side.

The Threat Of Nuclear War

In recent months, both in your country and mine, there has been renewed public concern about the threat of nuclear war and the arms buildup. I know it is not easy, especially for the German people, to live in the gale of intimidation that blows from the East. If I might quote Heine again, he almost foretold the fears of nuclear war when he wrote: "Wild, dark times are rumbling toward us, and the prophet who wishes to write a new apocalypse will have to invent entirely new beasts, and beasts so terrible that the ancient animal symbols ... will seem like cooing doves and cupids in comparison."

The nuclear threat is a terrible beast. Perhaps the banner carried in one of the nuclear demonstrations here in Germany said it best. The sign read, "I am afraid." I know of no Western leader who doesn't sympathize with that earnest plea. To those who march for peace, my heart is with you. I would be at the head of your parade if I believed marching alone could bring about a more secure world. And to the 2,800 women in Filderstadt who sent a petition for peace to President Brezhnev and myself, let me say I, myself, would sign your petition if I thought it could bring about harmony. I understand your genuine concerns.

The women of Filderstadt and I share the same goal. The question is how to proceed. We must think through the consequences of how we reduce the dangers to peace. Those who advocate that we unilaterally forego the modernization of our forces must prove that this will enhance our security and lead to moderation by the other side—in short, that it will advance, rather than undermine, the preservation of the peace. The weight of recent history does not support this notion.

Those who demand that we renounce the use of a crucial element of our deterrent strategy must show how this would decrease the likelihood of war. It is only by comparison with a nuclear war that the suffering caused by conventional war seems a lesser evil. Our goal must be to deter war of any kind.

And to those who decry the failure of arms control efforts to achieve substantial results must consider where the fault lies. I would remind them it is the United States that has proposed to ban land-based intermediate-range nuclear missiles—the missiles most threatening Europe. It is the United States that has proposed and will pursue deep cuts in strategic systems. It is the West that has long sought the detailed exchanges of information on forces and effective verification procedures. And it is dictatorships, not democracies, that need militarism to control their own people and impose their system on others.

Western Commitment To Arms Control

We in the West—Germans, Americans, our other allies—are deeply committed to continuing efforts to restrict the arms competition. Common sense demands that we persevere. I invite those who genuinely seek effective and lasting arms control to stand behind the far-reaching proposals that we have put forward. In return I pledge that we will sustain the closest of consultations with our allies.

On November 18th, I outlined a broad and ambitious arms control program. One element calls for reducing land-based intermediate-range nuclear missiles to zero on each side. If carried out, it would eliminate the growing threat to Western Europe posed by the U.S.S.R.'s modern SS-20 rockets, and it would make unnecessary the NATO decision to deploy American intermediate-range systems. And, by the way, I cannot understand why, among some, there is a greater fear of weapons which NATO is to deploy than of weapons the Soviet Union already has deployed. Our proposal is fair because it imposes equal limits and obligations on both sides and it calls for significant reductions, not merely a capping of an existing high level of destructive power. As you know, we have made this proposal in Geneva, where negotiations have been underway since the end of November last year. We intend to pursue those negotiations intensively. I regard them as a significant test of the Soviets' willingness to enter into meaningful arms control agreements.

On May 9th, we proposed to the Soviet Union that Strategic Arms Reduction Talks begin this month in Geneva. The U.S.S.R. has agreed, and talks will begin on June 29th. We in the United States want to focus on the most destabilizing systems, and thus reduce the risk of war. That is why in the first phase we propose to reduce substantially the number of ballistic missile warheads and the missiles themselves. In the second phase we will seek an equal ceiling on other elements of our strategic forces, including ballistic missile throw-weight, at less than current American levels. We will handle cruise missiles and bombers in an equitable fashion. We will negotiate in good faith and undertake these talks with the same seriousness of purpose that has marked our preparations over the last several months.

Another element of the program I outlined was a call for reductions in conventional forces in Europe. From the earliest postwar years, the Western democracies have faced the ominous reality that massive Soviet conventional forces would remain stationed where they do not belong. The muscle of Soviet forces in Central Europe far exceeds legitimate defense needs. Their presence is made more threatening still by a military doctrine that emphasizes mobility and surprise attack. And as history shows, these troops have built a legacy of intimidation and repression.

In response, the NATO allies must show they have the will and capacity to deter any conventional attack or any attempt to intimidate us. Yet we also will continue the search for responsible ways to reduce NATO and Warsaw Pact military personnel to equal levels.

In recent weeks, we in the alliance have consulted on how best to invigorate the Vienna negotiations on mutual and balanced force reductions. Based on these consultations, Western representatives in the Vienna talks soon will make a proposal by which the two alliances would reduce their respective ground force personnel in verifiable stages to a total of 700,000 men and their combined ground and air force personnel to a level of 900,000 men.

While the agreement would not eliminate the threat nor spare our citizens the task of maintaining a substantial defensive force, it could constitute a major step toward a safer Europe for both East and West. It could lead to military stability at lower levels and lessen the dangers of miscalculation and of surprise attack. And it also would demonstrate the political will of the two alliances to enhance stability by limiting their forces in the central area of their military competition.

The West has established a clear set of goals. We as an alliance will press forward with plans to improve our own conventional forces in Europe. At the same time, we propose an arms control agreement to equalize conventional forces at a significantly lower level.

We will move ahead with our preparations to modernize our nuclear forces in Europe. But, again, we also will work unceasingly to gain acceptance in Geneva of our proposal to ban land-based intermediate-range nuclear missiles.

In the United States, we will move forward with the plans I announced last year to modernize our strategic nuclear forces, which play so vital a role in maintaining peace by deterring war. Yet we also have proposed that Strategic Arms Reduction Talks begin, and we will pursue them determinedly.

The Need For Unity

In each of these areas our policies are based on the conviction that a stable military balance at the lowest possible level will help further the cause of peace. The other side will respond in good faith to these initiatives only if it believes we are resolved to provide for our own defense. Unless convinced that we will unite and stay united behind these arms control initiatives and modernization programs, our adversaries will seek to divide us from one another and our peoples from their leaders.

I am optimistic about our relationship with the Soviet Union if the Western nations remain true to their values and true to each other. I believe in Western civilization and in its moral power. I believe deeply in the principles the West esteems. And guided by these ideals, I believe we can find a no-nonsense, workable, and lasting policy that will keep the peace.

Earlier I said that the German people had built a remarkable cathedral of democracy. But we still have other work ahead. We must build a cathedral of peace, where nations are safe from war and where people need not fear for their liberties. I've heard the history of the famous cathedral at Cologne—how those beautiful soaring spires miraculously survived the destruction all around them, including part of the church itself.

Let us build a cathedral as the people of Cologne built theirs— with the deepest commitment and determination. Let us build as they did—not just for ourselves but for the generations beyond. For if we construct our peace properly, it will endure as long as the spires of Cologne.

36

Address by President Reagan to the People of Berlin, June 11, 1982

President Reagan visiting Allied Checkpoint Charlie with Governing Mayor Richard von Weizsäcker (left) and Chancellor Schmidt (right), West Berlin, June 11, 1982.

During his stay in Berlin, on June 11, 1982, President Reagan addressed Berliners assembled in front of the Charlottenburg Palace:

It was one of Germany's greatest sons, Goethe, who said that "there is strong shadow where there is much light." In our times, Berlin, more than any other place in the world, is such a meeting place of light and shadow, tyranny and freedom. To be here is truly to stand on freedom's edge and in the shadow of a wall that has come to symbolize all that is darkest in the world today, to sense how shining and priceless—and how much in need of constant vigilance and protection our legacy of liberty is.

This day marks a happy return for us. We paid our first visit to this great city more than three years ago, as private citizens. As with every other citizen of Berlin or visitor to Berlin, I came away with a vivid impression of a city that is more than a place on the map—a city that is a testament to what is both most inspiring and most troubling about the time we live in.

Thomas Mann once wrote that "A man lives not only his personal life as an individual, but also consciously or unconsciously the life of his epoch." Nowhere is this more true than in Berlin where each moment of everyday life is spent against the backdrop of contending global systems and ideas. To be a Berliner is to live the great historic struggle of this age, the latest chapter in man's timeless quest for freedom.

As Americans, we understand this. Our commitment to Berlin is a lasting one. Thousands of our citizens have served here since the first small contingent of American troops arrived on July 4, 1945, the anniversary of our independence as a nation. Americans have served here ever since—not as conquerors but as guardians of the freedom of West Berlin and its brave, proud, people.

Today I want to pay tribute to my fellow countrymen, military and civilian, who serve their country and the people of Berlin and, in so doing, stand as sentinals of freedom everywhere. I also wish to pay my personal respects to the people of this great city. My visit here today is proof that this American commitment has been worthwhile. Our freedom is indivisible.

The American commitment to Berlin is much deeper than our military presence here. In the 37 years since World War II, a succession of American Presidents has made it clear that our role in Berlin is emblematic of our larger search for peace throughout Europe and the world. Ten years ago this month, that search brought into force the Quadrapartite Agreement on Berlin. A decade later, West Berliners live more securely, can travel more freely and, most significantly, have more contact with friends and relatives in East Berlin and East Germany than was possible ten years ago. These achievements reflect the realistic approach of Allied negotiators who recognized that practical progress can be made even while basic differences remain between East and West.

As a result—as a result, both sides have managed to handle their differences in Berlin without the clash of arms, to the benefit of all mankind. The United States remains committed to the Berlin Agreement. We will continue to expect strict observance and full implementation in all aspects of this accord, including those which apply to the Eastern Sector of Berlin. But if we are heartened by the partial progress achieved in Berlin, other developments made us aware of the growing military power and expansionism of the Soviet Union.

Instead of working with the West to reduce tensions and erase the danger of war, the Soviet Union is engaged in the greatest military build-up in the history of the world. It has used its new-found might to ruthlessly pursue its goals around the world. As the sad case of Afghanistan proves, the Soviet Union has not always respected the precious right of national sovereignty it is committed to uphold as a signatory of the United Nations Charter. And only one day's auto ride from here, in the great city of Warsaw, a courageous people suffer because they dare to strive for the very fundamental human rights which the Helsinki final act proclaimed.

The citizens of free Berlin appreciate better than anyone the importance of allied unity in the face of such challenges. Ten years after the Berlin Agreement, the hope it engendered for lasting peace remains a hope rather than a certainty. But the hopes of free people—be they German or American—are stubborn things. We will not be lulled or bullied into fatalism, into resignation. We believe that progress for just and lasting peace can be made—that substantial areas of agreement can be reached with potential adversaries—when the forces of freedom act with firmness, unity and a sincere willingness to negotiate.

To succeed at the negotiating table, we allies have learned that a healthy military balance is a necessity. Yesterday, the other NATO heads of government and I agreed that it is essential to preserve and strengthen such a military balance. And let there be no doubt: the United States will continue to honor its commitment to Berlin.

Our forces will remain here as long as necessary to preserve the peace and protect the freedom of the people of Berlin. For us the American presence in Berlin, as long as it is needed, is not a burden. It is a sacred trust.

Ours is a defensive mission. We pose no threat to those who live on the other side of the Wall. But we do extend a challenge—a new Berlin initiative to the leaders of the Soviet Bloc. It is a challenge for peace. We challenge the men in the Kremlin to join with us in the quest for peace, security, and a lowering of the tensions and weaponry that could lead to future conflict.

We challenge the Soviet Union, as we proposed last year, to eliminate their SS-20, SS-4, and SS-5 missiles. If Chairman Brezhnev agrees to this, we stand ready to forego all of our ground-launched cruise missiles and Pershing II missiles.

We challenge the Soviet Union, as NATO proposed yesterday, to slash the conventional ground forces of the Warsaw Pact and NATO in Central Europe to 700,000 men each and the total ground and air forces of the two alliances to 900,000 men each. And we challenge the Soviet Union to live up to its signature its leader placed on the Helsinki Treaty so that the basic human rights of Soviet and Eastern Europe people will be respected.

A positive response to these sincere and reasonable points from the Soviets, these calls for conciliation instead of confrontation, could open the door for a conference on disarmament in Europe.

We Americans—we Americans are optimists, but we are also realists. We're a peaceful people, but we're not a weak or gullible people. So we look with hope to the Soviet Union's response. But we expect positive actions rather than rhetoric as the first proof of Soviet good intentions. We expect that the response to my Berlin initiative for peace will demonstrate finally that the Soviet Union is serious about working to reduce tensions in other parts of the world as they have been able to do here in Berlin.

Peace, it has been said, is more than the absence of armed conflict. Reducing military forces alone will not automatically guarantee the long-term prospects of peace.

Several times in the 1950's and '60's the world went to the brink of war over Berlin. Those confrontations did not come because of military forces or operations alone. They arose because the Soviet Union rfused to allow the free flow of peoples and ideas between East and West. And they came because the Soviet authorities and their minions repressed millions of citizens in Eastern Germany who did not wish to live under a communist dictatorship.

So I want to concentrate the second part of America's new Berlin initiative on ways to reduce the human barriers—barriers as bleak and brutal as the Berlin Wall itself—which divide Europe today.

If I had only one message to urge on the leaders of the Soviet Bloc, it would be this: Think of your own coming generations. Look with me ten years into the future when we will celebrate the 20th anniversary of the Berlin Agreement. What then will be the fruits of our efforts? Do the Soviet leaders want to be remembered for a prison wall, ringed with barbed wire and armed guards whose weapons are aimed at innocent civilians—their own civilians? Do they want to conduct themselves in a way that will earn only the contempt of free peoples and the distrust of their own citizens?

Or do they want to be remembered for having taken up our offer to use Berlin as a starting point for true efforts to reduce the human and political divisions which are the ultimate cause of every war.

We in the West have made our choice. America and our allies welcome peaceful competition in ideas, in economics and in all facets of human activity. We seek no advantage. We covet no territory. And we wish to force no ideology or way of life on others.

The time has come, 10 years after the Berlin agreement, to fulfill the promise it seemed to offer at its dawn. I call on President Brezhnev to join me in a sincere effort to translate the dashed hopes of the 1970s into the reality of a safer and freer Europe in the 1980s.

I am determined to assure that our civilization averts the catastrophe of a nuclear war. Stability depends primarily on the maintenance of a military balance which offers no temptation to an aggressor. And the arms control proposals which I have made are designed to enhance deterrence and achieve stability at substantially lower and equal force levels. At the same time, other measures might be negotiated between the United States and the Soviet Union to reinforce the peace and help reduce the possibility of a nuclear conflict. These include measures to enhance mutual confidence and to improve communication both in time of peace and in a crisis.

Past agreements have created a hot line between Moscow and Washington, established measures to reduce the danger of nuclear accidents, and provided for notification of some missile launches. We are now studying other concrete and practical steps to help further reduce the risk of a nuclear conflict which I intend to explore with the Soviet Union.

It is time we went further to avert the risk of war through accidents or misunderstanding.

We shortly will approach the Soviet Union with proposals in such areas as notification of strategic exercises, of missile launches and expanded exchange of strategic forces data. Taken together, these steps would represent a qualitative improvement in the nuclear environment. They would help reduce the chances of misinterpretation in the case of exercises and test launches. And they would reduce the secrecy and ambiguity which surround military activity. We are considering additional measures as well.

We will be making these proposals in good faith to the Soviet Union. We hope that their response to this Berlin initiative, so appropriate to a city that is acutely conscious of the costs and risks of war, will be positive.

A united, resolute Western Alliance stands ready to defend itself if necessary. But we are also ready to work with the Soviet bloc in peaceful cooperation if the leaders of the East are willing to respond in kind.

Let them remember the message of Schiller that only "He who has done his best for his own time has lived for all times." Let them join with us in our time to achieve a lasting peace and a better life for tomorrow's generations on both sides of that blighted wall. And let the Brandenburg Gate become a symbol not of two separate and hostile worlds, but an open door through which ideas, free ideas and peaceful competition flourish.

My final message is for the people of Berlin. Even before my first visit to your city, I felt a part of you, as all free men and women around the world do. We lived through the blockade and airlift with you. We witnessed the heroic reconstruction of a devastated city and we watched the creation of your strong democratic institutions.

When I came here in 1978, I was deeply moved and proud of your success. What finer proof of what freedom can accomplish than the vibrant, prosperous island you've created in the midst of a hostile sea? Today, my reverence for your courage and accomplishment has grown even deeper.

You are a constant inspiration for us all—for our hopes and ideals, and for the human qualities of courage, endurance and faith that are the one secret weapon of the West no totalitarian regime can ever match. As long as Berlin exists, there can be no doubt about the hope for democracy.

Yes, the hated Wall still stands. But taller and stronger than that bleak barrier dividing East from West, free from oppressed, stands the character of the Berliners themselves.

You have endured in your splendid city on the Spree, and my return visit has convinced me, in the words of the beloved old song that "Berlin bleibt doch Berlin"—Berlin is still Berlin.

We all remember John Kennedy's stirring words when he visited Berlin. I can only add that we in America and in the West are still Berliners, too, and always will be. And I am proud to say today that it is good to be home again.

God bless you. Dankeschön.

37

Remarks by President Reagan and Chancellor Kohl on the Chancellor's Arrival in Washington, November 15, 1982

Chancellor Kohl and President Reagan during welcoming ceremony at the White House, Washington, November 15, 1982.

On Nov. 15, 1982, Chancellor Helmut Kohl (who succeeded Chancellor Schmidt on Oct. 1, 1982) paid his first official visit to the U.S. Remarks exchanged by President Reagan and Chancellor Kohl at the welcoming ceremony on the South Lawn of the White House on Nov. 15, 1982, were as follows:

The President.

Chancellor Kohl, Mrs. Kohl, on behalf of the American people, Nancy and I are honored and delighted to welcome you to Washington. Before my visit to the Federal Republic of Germany earlier this year, Chancellor Kohl, who had not yet attained the high office he now holds, helped organize several rallies. He wanted to let us know that we were welcome and to reassure all Americans of the sincere goodwill of the German people.

Chancellor Kohl, I appreciated very much that magnificent gesture. I understand that in Bonn where some 75,000 people attended the rally, one of the banners read "Say Something Good About America." Well, today it certainly makes all Americans happy to repay this compliment because there are many good things to say about you, Mr. Chancellor, about the German people and about the strong bond that unites us.

A recent study has revealed that today more Americans trace their ancestry to your country than to any other nation. German immigrants provided the hard work and determination that settled much of the Midwest, taking rugged frontier land like that in the Dakotas and reaping from it bountiful harvests that helped feed the world. In other industries, German energy and German ingenuity helped build the factories and firms that catapulted our standard of living and elevated the lot of the common man from a life of drudgery to new progress consistent with individual dignity and respect. But, as you are aware, Mr. Chancellor, it wasn't simply hard work that built America. It was freedom available here— freedom to which German immigrants greatly contributed.

One of the first precedents for freedom of press, for example, was established when Peter Zenger, a German immigrant, spoke out in his newspaper, against the abuse of power by a public official. When the jury freed Zenger, they were laying freedom of press as a cornerstone of our democratic system. In the middle of the 19th century, when turmoil was sweeping through Western Europe, we were the recipient of many political exiles who made significant contributions to American liberty. One of the most remarkable, Carl Schurz was one of the original members of the Republican party. Now, you see one reason why I personally am so grateful, Mr. Chancellor.

With us today to greet you is a group of young people from your country who are spending the autumn months living with American families in Virginia. They're part of our Youth Exchange Project between our two countries, and these kinds of ties bode well for the future.

The future of both our nations depends so much on friendship and the values we share. In these uncertain times when a power to the East has built a massive war machine far in excess of any legitimate defensive needs, the Western democracies must stand firmly together if our freedom and peace of the world are to be preserved.

165

The German people are on the front lines of freedom. When I was in your country a few months ago I told your citizens, "You are not alone. We are with you." Well, today, Mr. Chancellor, I can tell you we're happy that the German people are with us.

The Western democracies, the future freedom of mankind, and the peace of the world would be far less secure if it were not so. Your personal commitment and that of your government to the needs of our alliance are well appreciated here, as is the depth which you add to the meaning of our covenant. In truth, as you recently observed, we are not a military alliance. The community of arms, you said, is there to defend the community of ideas. The important point is that we have common ideas regarding human rights, civil rights, our moral values, our moral laws.

I look forward to our talks today. As I would expect that a meeting of the leaders of the two great nations whose interests are so intertwined, there are many vital issues to discuss. As all good friends do, we will disagree at times, but in free societies we're accustomed to differences and also to a peaceful resolution to achieve our common goals.

As we stand here today, I am confident that our shared interests, our common vision of the future and our joint commitment to human freedom will overcome any differences between our countries. Our governments will work in the closest consultation, in a spirit of amity and straightforwardness.

We thank you for coming and, in the name of the people of the United States, wilkommen. [*Applause.*]

The Chancellor. Mr. President, Mrs. Reagan,
ladies and gentlemen:

I thank you, Mr. President, most warmly for the very kind words of welcome and for the warmhearted reception we have been given here.

On the 7th of April, 1953, almost 30 years ago, the Chancellor of the Federal Republic of Germany stood here for the first time. And on that occasion, Konrad Adenauer said that we Germans are loyal partners on the road to freedom and peace, a road on which the United States is ahead of all other nations.

Mr. President, I want you and all citizens of the United States to know that these remarks by Chancellor Adenauer still hold true today and will do so in the future as well. The Federal Republic of Germany is and will remain a loyal partner of the United States of America.

Recent opinion polls have shown, once more, that in the Federal Republic of Germany there is wide-based firm confidence

166

in the Atlantic partnership. And to all Americans, therefore, I say today, most emphatically, you can count on your German friends.

The North Atlantic Alliance and our friendship with the United States are the foundation of our active policy for safeguarding peace in freedom.

The real strength of our alliance does not derive solely from the number of troops and weapons. Our alliance is strong because the citizens of 16 North American and European countries have a common goal. They are determined to safeguard the freedom, the common heritage and civilization of their peoples founded on the principles of democracy, individual liberty, and the rule of law. This goal is laid down in the preamble to the North Atlantic Treaty.

We must constantly remind ourselves and in particular our young fellow citizens of these foundations of our equal partnership and of our deep friendship because our shared fundamental convictions are the key to unity. And from unity ensues the strength to attain our goals, to safeguard peace and freedom through firmness and the readiness for negotiation; to ensure economic and social stability; and to cooperate fairly and constructively with the countries of the Third World.

Despite domestic changes in our countries and changes of government, eight American Presidents and six German Chancellors have contributed towards German-American partnership. For us Germans, gratitude, too, is an element of our friendship with America.

My generation, my wife and I, know from our experience that after terrible war, when we were still children and pupils and students, the Americans saved us not only from hunger.

We have not forgotten what the Hoover aid program and what the Quaker aid program and the CARE parcel gifts action meant for us at that time. The Americans helped us to build a free state and our Constitution, especially the Catalog of Basic Rights, owes much to the American experience of democracy. Today there are 245,000 American troops and their families in our country where they are welcome guests. These troops serve together with 500,000 members of the Bundeswehr and the forces of five other allied countries. What clearer proof could there be, Mr. President, that we are dependent on one another? The more than 50 million American citizens of German descent also constitute a strong bond of friendship between Germany and the United States. And I convey particularly warm regards to all of them today on my first visit to Washington as Federal Chancellor.

Next year will mark the tricentennial of the first wave of German immigrants to America, and to mark this occasion, Germans and Americans intend to hold a big celebration together. We will recall our common origins and from this path draw strength, courage, and confidence for our common future.

Mr. President, let us make the forthcoming anniversary the start of a period of particularly close, intensive, and fruitful German-American cooperation. Let us start here and now. I am looking forward to this cooperation.

Thank you very much.

38

Joint Statement by President Reagan and Chancellor Kohl, November 16, 1982

Both parties issued the following joint statement at the conclusion of their discussions:

During the visit of the Chancellor of the Federal Republic of Germany, Helmut Kohl, he and President Reagan held detailed talks in Washington on current political and economic issues on November 15, 1982. The Chancellor is also meeting with Secretary of State Shultz, Secretary of Defense Weinberger, Secretary of the Treasury Regan, high-ranking Administration officials, and leading members of the Senate.

The discussions attested to the depth and the breadth of German-American friendship. The United States and the Federal Republic of Germany are partners as well as friends, sharing common ideals, human and democratic values. In today's uncertain world, this commitment has become more important than ever. Our shared values form the unshakeable foundation for our joint efforts to maintain the freedom and prosperity of the Western world.

The discussions were based on a determination to work together as closely as possible to meet the challenges of the closing decades of the twentieth century.

These challenges are as critical as those which faced the great statesmen who founded our partnership more than three decades ago. During the past thirty years the Atlantic partnership has been successful in guaranteeing to our peoples more freedom, security, and prosperity than at any time in history. The President and the Chancellor reaffirmed during their discussions their common view on the central role played by the Atlantic Alliance in the foreign policies of their respective governments.

A major reason for success of the Atlantic Alliance has been the close relationship which has developed between the United States and the Federal Republic of Germany. German-American ties are deeper than simple calculations of national interest.

After World War II and after the destruction caused by it in Germany, these ties originated from the generous humanitarian aid and the political support which the United States granted to the German people and their young democracy. German-American relations are based on a close affection among our two peoples and are supported by intimate personal and familial ties between Americans and Germans. Ours is a relationship based on mutual support and open discussion between equal partners.

During the discussions it was agreed that high level consultations between the United States and the Federal Republic of Germany will be continued during a visit to Bonn by Secretary of State Shultz in early December.

An example of the close ties between our two nations are the more than fifty million Americans of German descent. German Americans have provided major contributions to every aspect of American life and form one of the foundations of American society. The President and the Chancellor anticipated with pleasure the joint celebration in 1983 of the Tricentennial of German immigration to the United States. President Reagan announced today the formation of a Presidential commission to help prepare American commemoration of this important event. Chancellor Kohl described plans for celebrations in the Federal Republic of Germany. They stressed that the Tricentennial should be a joint celebration among the peoples of their two nations and reaffirmed the intention of President Reagan and President Carstens to meet in the United States in October, 1983, to highlight the American celebration.

The wider the understanding of the commonality of the issues facing the United States and the Federal Republic of Germany, the stronger our partnership will become. For this reason President Reagan and Chancellor Kohl were pleased to reaffirm their support for the initiatives to broaden US-German contacts and to set up a multilateral youth exchange among Western industrialized democracies. The purpose is to pass on to the younger generations in our nations the sense of partnership which the older generation feels so deeply.

The President and the Chancellor reaffirmed the Alliance's overall concept for successfully safeguarding peace in Europe as embodied in the declaration made by the heads of state and government of the Atlantic Alliance in Bonn on June 10, 1982. As stressed in that declaration, they agreed that in accordance with current NATO defense plans, and within the context of NATO strategy and its triad of forces, they will continue to strengthen NATO's defense posture, with special regard to conventional forces.

The Alliance has demonstrated that it serves the cause of peace and freedom. Even in difficult situations, it has been able to do so because its members have acted in a spirit of solidarity. The Alliance does not threaten anyone. Nor does it aspire to superiority, but in the interests of peace it cannot accept inferiority either. Its aim is, as before, to prevent any war and safeguard peace and freedom. None of the weapons of the Alliance will ever be used except in response to attack.

The Chancellor paid tribute to the crucial contribution that the United States renders to the joint security of the Alliance through the indispensable presence of American troops in Europe. The President and the Chancellor agreed that a unilateral reduction of American troops would have a destabilizing effect and, at the same time, would undermine efforts for negotiated force reductions.

The President expressed his great appreciation for the significant and uninterrupted German contribution to the common defense. In particular, he paid tribute to the German-American agreement of April 15, 1982 on Wartime Host Nation Support, which entails considerable additional expenditure by the Federal Republic of Germany and the United States of America for common defense.

The President and the Chancellor stressed the need for close, comprehensive, and timely consultations to strengthen the Alliance's cohesion and its capacity to act. They attached particular importance to German-American cooperation. They hoped that informal meetings of the foreign ministers of the Alliance would be continued.

The President welcomed the resolve of the Government of the Federal Republic of Germany to strengthen European unification. The President and the Chancellor paid tribute to the important role of the European Community and all its member states for economic and political stability in Europe and the world. The development of a united Europe will strengthen cooperation between Europe and the United States and, hence, also reinforce the Alliance.

The President and the Chancellor paid tribute to the close agreement and cooperation between the Federal Republic of Germany and the Three Powers in all matters relating to Berlin and Germany as a whole. They concurred in the view that the preservation of trouble-free conditions in and around Berlin was an essential element of East-West relations and of the international situation as a whole.

The President reaffirmed American support for the political aim of the Federal Republic of Germany to work for a state of peace in Europe in which the German nation will regain its unity through free self-determination.

A major subject discussed during the meetings was relations with the Soviet Union. The values and goals of the Soviet Union do not correspond to our own. The USSR restricts freedom on its own territory and in countries under its influence, and has shown that it is ready to use force or the threat of force to achieve its foreign policy aims. Security of Western societies requires constant attention to the military threat posed by the USSR. The Federal Republic of Germany and the United States of America gear their policies in East-West relations to the concept of renunciation of force, human rights, and the right of nations to self-determination.

The President and the Chancellor called upon the Soviet Union to comply with internationally recognized rules of conduct. This required respect for the principles enshrined in the Charter of the United Nations and in the Helsinki Final Act as well as a worldwide policy of moderation and restraint.

In this spirit, the President and the Chancellor underlined their desire to improve relations with the Soviet Union. They are ready to conduct relations with the new leadership in Moscow with the aim of extending areas of cooperation to their mutual benefit if Soviet conduct makes that possible. It is especially important at present for the West to approach the Soviet Union with a clear, steadfast and coherent attitude which combines the defense of its own interests with the readiness to pursue constructive relations, dialogue, and cooperation with the leadership of the Soviet Union.

In this regard, the President and the Chancellor greeted with satisfaction the recent agreement on measures leading to a broader consensus on East-West economic relations. They attached the greatest importance to a common Allied approach to this issue. Close consultation and cooperation on East-West economic issues is as vital to Western interests as is the traditional cooperation on political and security questions.

It is the purpose of our common efforts that trade with the Soviet Union and Eastern Europe should be conducted on the basis of a balance of mutual advantages. While noting the important part which our economic relations with the Warsaw Pact countries can play in the development of a stable East-West relationship, the President and the Chancellor agreed that those relations should be approached in a prudent and diversified manner, consistent with our political and security interests.

The Chancellor expressed his appreciation for the lifting of the embargo on oil and gas technology and equipment, which he considered as evidence of successful efforts on the part of all concerned for improved coordination of Western policy in the economic field.

The President and the Chancellor agreed that developments in Poland, which continued to cause great concern, had an adverse effect on efforts to promote security and cooperation in Europe. They drew attention once more to the Soviet Union's responsibility for the events in Poland. They called upon the Polish leadership to lift martial law in Poland, to release all detainees, to reverse the ban on the trade union Solidarity and, through serious dialogue with the Church and appointed workers' representatives, to seek national consensus which is the only way to lead Poland out of its present crisis, free from any external interference. They hoped that the release of Lech Walesa will promote these objectives. The President and the Chancellor welcomed the numerous intiatives for humanitarian aid for the Polish people. They agreed that this aid should be stepped up wherever possible.

The President and the Chancellor agreed on the importance of the CSCE process initiated by the Helsinki Final Act and advocated that it be continued. It is a long-term process which has been gravely affected by events in Poland. It can prove successful only if the participating countries observe the principles and provisions of the Final Act in their entirety. They expressed support for the new proposals, responsive to events in Poland and the USSR, put forward by the West in the resumed Madrid session, as reasonable and essential elements of a balanced outcome.

The President and the Chancellor agreed that the CSCE review conference, which was resumed in Madrid on November 9, 1982, should agree on a substantive and balanced final document which leads to progress in the important humanitarian field of East-West relations and contains a precise mandate for a Conference on Disarmament in Europe (CDE), envisaging militarily significant confidence and security building measures covering the whole of Europe, from the Atlantic to the Urals.

The President and the Chancellor noted that arms control and disarmament as well as defense and deterrence were integral parts of NATO'S security policy. They agreed that significant progress towards reduction of the levels of nuclear and conventional forces through balanced and verifiable agreements would be an important contribution to the reduction of international tensions. The incessant unilateral increase in Soviet armaments in recent years has threatened the security of the Alliance and international stability and made even more urgent the need to establish a balance of forces between East and West. The goal of the United States and the Federal Republic of Germany remains to achieve a stable balance of both nuclear and conventional forces at the lowest possible level.

The President and the Chancellor recalled the comprehensive program of arms control proposals put forward by the United States on the basis of close consultation and adopted by the entire Alliance at the Bonn Summit on June 10, 1982. They stressed their common belief that this program provides the best hope for true reductions in arsenals of both intermediate and intercontinental strategic weapons. They rejected the proposals to freeze existing levels of nuclear weapons, or for one-sided reductions by the West, as inadequate for substantive arms control and as harmful to the security of the Atlantic Alliance. They noted also that the Soviet Union had in recent years refused to reciprocate the unilateral restraint in this field by the United States. They expressed the strong judgement that true reductions in nuclear armaments would be possible only when the Soviet Union is convinced of the determination of the West to maintain its defenses at the level necessary to meet the threat posed by massive increases in Soviet nuclear forces.

In this connection they attached particular importance to negotiations on reductions of strategic arms and of intermediate range nuclear forces now underway between the United States and the Soviet Union in Geneva. President Reagan reaffirmed his determination to do his utmost to achieve true reductions in nuclear armaments through balanced and verifiable agreements. The President and the Chancellor pointed out that negotiations in Geneva are serious and substantial. At the same time they expressed concern at the refusal of the Soviet Union to take into account legitimate Western security concerns.

In conformity with their policy for actively safeguarding peace through firmness and negotiation, the President and the Chancellor reaffirmed their commitment to both parts of the NATO dual-track decision of December 12, 1979, consisting of a program of INF modernization and an offer to the Soviet Union of arms control negotiations on INF. An important aspect of Western security policy remains the common determination to deploy modernized longer-range INF missiles in Europe beginning at the end of 1983 if negotiations on this subject now underway in Geneva do not result in a concrete agreement making deployment unnecessary. The President and the Chancellor noted that the decision to deploy the systems in Europe was based on a unanimous finding by members of the Atlantic Alliance that increases in Soviet weapons, in particular introduction of SS-20 missiles, had endangered the security of Western Europe and thus of the entire Alliance. They stressed that the complete elimination of Soviet and United States land-based, longer-range INF missiles, as proposed by the United States, would be an equitable and fair result and would be a substantial contribution to serious arms control. They called upon the Soviet Union to negotiate seriously toward this end. The Chancellor restated his full confidence in the American negotiating effort in Geneva and welcomed the close and continuous process of consultations within the Alliance.

President Reagan described the ideas behind his Berlin initiative of June 10, 1982 for an agreement between the United States and the Soviet Union on measures to help avoid the danger that accident or miscalculation could lead to a nuclear exchange between East and West. He stated that the United States was preparing proposals for nuclear confidence-building measures which would be presented by American representatives at the Geneva negotiations. The Chancellor and the President expressed their hope that the Soviet Union would join with the United States in progressing rapidly to an agreement on such measures. They also remain committed to halting the spread of nuclear weapons through the pursuit of vigorous non-proliferation policies.

The President and the Chancellor underscored their undiminished interest in substantial reduction in conventional forces in central Europe. They recalled the new draft treaty which the Western participants had presented at the Vienna negotiations on mutual and balanced force reductions. This proposal provides an excellent foundation for a balanced agreement on reduction of conventional forces in Europe. The President and the Chancellor called upon Warsaw Pact participants to react positively.

They stated that agreement on a comprehensive and fully verifiable ban on chemical weapons in the Geneva Committee on Disarmament remained a prime objective of their policies.

They also attached great importance to efforts in the United Nations to secure transparency by promoting military openness, verification, and wider availability of information on defense spending.

The President and the Chancellor were in complete agreement on the requirement for special attention to Alliance needs on the Southern Flank. They emphasized in this connection their resolve to support the Turkish Government in its efforts to lead Turkey back to democracy.

The President and the Chancellor expressed confidence that our free societies would overcome the current difficult economic situation. They attached paramount importance to restoring the conditions for sustained growth through higher investments, in order to reduce unemployment and to maintain price stability.

The economic policies of industrial nations must be closely coordinated. Each country must bear in mind the effects that its political and economic measures will have on other countries. These factors will also have an important effect on the Economic Summit to be held in Williamsburg at the invitation of the United States. Both sides reaffirmed the importance of conducting the discussions at this summit on the basis of openness, trust, and informality.

The President and the Chancellor discussed the dangers posed by rising protectionism to world trade and the economic well-being of nations. They reaffirmed their commitment to the multilateral trading system, looking forward to a successful GATT Ministerial meeting in Geneva this month.

The President and the Chancellor agreed that it is imperative to respect and promote the independence of the countries of the Third World and that genuine nonalignment is an important element of stability and world peace. The President and the Chancellor reaffirmed their readiness to continue to cooperate with Third World countries on the basis of equal partnership.

The continuing Soviet occupation of Afghanistan is a strain on international relations. The President and the Chancellor deplored the fact that the Soviet Union continued to defy international opinion and ignored United Nations' resolutions calling for the withdrawal of foreign troops from Afghanistan, as well as the right to self-determination for Afghanistan and restoration of its nonaligned status. Afghanistan remains an acid test of Soviet readiness to respect the independence, autonomy, and genuine nonalignment of Third World countries and to exercise restraint in its international behavior.

The Chancellor welcomed President Reagan's proposal of September 1, 1982 as a realistic attempt to promote the peace process in the Middle East. They agreed that negotiations between Israel and its neighbors in the framework of UN resolutions 242 and 338 offer the best opportunity for peaceful resolution of disputes in that area. The United States and the Federal Republic of Germany, together with its partners in European Political Cooperation, will, as before, seek to ensure that the American and European efforts for a comprehensive, just, and lasting peace in the Middle East, on the basis of existing achievements, are complementary to each other. They called for early withdrawal of all foreign forces from Lebanon. They continued to urge that the sovereignty and unity of Lebanon be restored and expressed their support for the reconstruction of Lebanon.

39

Speech by Chancellor Kohl Before the American Council on Germany in New York, November 16, 1982

On November 16, 1982, in New York, Chancellor Kohl addressed members and guests of the American Council on Germany. Following introductory comments by Mr. John J. McCloy, Honorary Chairman of the Council, Chancellor Kohl stated:

I am delighted to be able to end my stay in the United States in your company and with an exchange of views with members and guests of the American Council on Germany. Thank you very much for the invitation to address this Council.

When Konrad Adenauer paid his first visit to the United States of America thirty years ago he said, on setting foot on American soil: "I believe that only very seldom in history has a victorious nation held out a helping hand to the defeated side in such a way as the American people have done. This munificence is manifest in every conceivable form: by the acts of individuals and organizations, by decisions of Congress and by measures of the U.S. Administration."

Let me today repeat those words of thanks expressed then by Konrad Adenauer on behalf of the German people to you, Mr. McCloy, both personally and as someone who represents many others. The German-American friendship that was reestablished on that occasion is still very much alive today.

We know what it means to us when the President of the United States says on German soil: "Europe's shores are our shores, Europe's borders are our borders, and Berlin's freedom is our freedom."

We also know what we are talking about when we say that the North Atlantic Alliance of free democratic countries has safeguarded peace for thirty years now and will continue to do so. And when I state that we Germans know this I mean the vast majority of my fellow countrymen. For this I do not need to cite the recent surveys in which 90 per cent of the people questioned were in favour of the Alliance, its defense capability, and close relations with your great country.

I also know that my fellow countrymen do not just regard German-American relations and our partnership in the Alliance in military terms. For us the Alliance is much more than a military association. It is a community in which free peoples work together to preserve what they cherish most dearly:

A life in freedom, human dignity and social justice. Good, dependable and calculable friends and allies.

In my policy statement to the German Bundestag I said that my country's foreign and security policy is founded on the North Atlantic Alliance and our friendship and partnership with the United States of America.

My policy is a policy for freedom, a policy for peace in Europe and throughout the world, a policy for human rights and against hunger and distress, a policy for the right of self-determination of the whole German nation in a united Europe.

These political principles can only be realized in alliance with our friends and partners, in the community of the free West. The Federal Republic of Germany is firmly rooted in that community. Everyone knows that any wavering on our part, situated as we are in the heart of Europe, would constitute a threat to our existence.

The strength and vitality of the Alliance derive from the realization of the members of the Alliance that they have to preserve and defend common values, from their political solidarity and from their readiness and ability to maintain an adequate military strength.

Our contribution to the deterrence of the Alliance is the Bundeswehr. These 500,000 well-trained and well-equipped troops can be increased in a very short time to 1,250,000. They are the core of foreward-defense in central Europe. My country is only able to render this contribution to NATO because young Germans are willing, as conscripts, to defend peace and freedom in their fatherland.

A nation that is not determined to defend itself will throw away its freedom and with it peace. Our forces know that they can only fulfill their mission of defending peace together with their fellow servicemen of our allies.

Over 400,000 servicemen from six NATO countries are already stationed in the Federal Republic of Germany in peacetime, 245,000 of them from the United States. Every one of them is welcome as a friend in my country. Every one of them should know that all Germans are grateful to them for helping to defend the peace and freedom of us all.

The despicable attacks on American military facilities in our country are isolated acts by terrorists.

We realize, too, that it is not easy for the United States, in view of its global commitments, to maintain this contribution undiminished. We are of course aware of what the United States is doing to protect our common vital interests outside Europe, to preserve the independence and security of the free world. Wherever we can and wherever we have the strength to do so we shall support the United States of America in this task of safeguarding the mutual interests of the free industrial countries.

The Federal Republic of Germany does a great deal to help in particular those NATO countries who play an important role on NATO's jeopardized Southern flank but who have not the resources to maintain this defense posture alone. After the United States we grant the most defense aid to Portugal, Turkey and Greece.

We give full backing to the Alliance's policy, the main elements of which are: equilibrium and defense capability, disarmament and arms control, dialogue and cooperation.

For the conditions of the future we need a strong Alliance capable of action which will permit the leading Western power to pursue a global policy aimed at safeguarding peace, stability and freedom for all nations.

No one should doubt our resolve to defend peace with all our strength. But neither should anyone doubt our will for dialogue, our urgent desire for arms control and disarmament, for negotiations on force reductions. We support both elements of the Alliance's dualtrack decision. We are fervently striving for a balance of military forces at the lowest possible level.

We do not want a policy of confrontation with the East. We do not want to build up enemies in our imagination. We intend to continue a realistic policy of understanding with the new Soviet leadership and with the East European countries. We shall continue to strive for genuine détente so as to make the division of Germany and Europe more tolerable.

This also includes the continuation of economic co-operation with Eastern Europe and the present policy of dialogue, especially at the CSCE follow-up meeting in Madrid.

In this context there have been setbacks, even serious ones. For instance there has been Afghanistan, and there have been the developments in Poland which we are following with great concern. In our dialogue with the Soviet Union we will not remain silent about these developments.

Let me mention a third commitment. We must constantly strive to strengthen the cohesion of the Alliance and pave the way for joint action.

Obviously, the interests of the sixteen members of the Alliance are not wholly consonant in all fields from the outset. But in one respect we are certain that you, too, fully appreciate that European unification, co-operation among the nations of Europe, the efforts to foster good-neighborly relations in Europe, help to strengthen the Western community and increase stability, not only in Europe. This also applies to the recent agreement with France to intensify consultations on security policy.

To achieve this, the negotiations in Geneva must be successfully completed. We very much want them to be a success. We do not doubt the serious resolve of the United States Government to achieve these results. We are in close contact with them on this matter. There is a chance that acceptable results can be achieved by the end of 1983 if the Soviet Union is willing to renounce its superiority of intermediate-range nuclear weapons, which is a threat to our security, and in this way to stabilize East-West relations. It must be made clear to the Soviet Union that successful negotiations alone can prevent arms modernization. It must realize that it cannot capitalize on fear. We will not allow the genuine will for peace among young people and the great moral commitment of the churches and social and political groups to be abused for the purpose of freezing the Soviet superiority resulting from an arms build-up and at the same time driving wedges into the Alliance.

Today it is no longer a question of help but of solidarity and responsibility for the world economy. Great pressure of an international economic crisis weighs upon all of us. In this context I very much welcome the fact that it has proved possible to lower interest rates in the United States, which are of worldwide importance. I hope that this development will be sustained.

Precisely in these difficult economic circumstances we must again and again turn to one another with the will to reach agreement. The recent steel arrangement between the European community and the United States shows that this is possible. The fact that we are able to work out a common overall concept for our economic relations with the East, with all being ready to make concessions, fills me with optimism and hope for our future relations.

Many a concession has been very painful for us too. I would mention the dramatic situation of our steel industry despite its considerable efforts to restructure and adapt itself. What is important, therefore, is that we have ultimately arrived at solutions which each of us can accept and which, taken as a whole, will make us stronger because they strengthen our cohesion.

The fact, that our relations are marked by discussion in a spirit of partnership leading to consensus is their very strength.

This also enables us jointly to find new responses to new challenges.

Partnership among free peoples calls for fresh efforts every day, but these efforts are indeed worthwhile.

40

Statement by Chancellor Kohl in Washington, April 15, 1983

President Reagan greeting Chancellor Kohl at the White House, Washington, April 15, 1983.

At the conclusion of his talks with President Reagan, Chancellor Kohl made the following statement on April 15, 1983:

First of all I would like to thank President Reagan for his invitation and the hospitality extended to us.

Our talks in which the two Foreign Ministers and our closest advisers participated, gave the President and myself an opportunity to continue our intensive and friendly dialogue which we began when I became Chancellor of the Federal Republic of Germany.

We had a good, cordial and open conversation among friends, about which I am highly pleased. This exchange has shown that beyond our personal understanding German-American partnership rests on a broad basis of shared values and interests.

We discussed in depth and in great earnest the essential aspects of our joint peace and disarmament policy. In the course of this year important issues are pending. We are profoundly interested in finding solutions to the issues at hand in agreement with the East.

This includes the Geneva negotiations on U.S. and Soviet intermediate-range missiles. We are agreed that the recent Western proposal offers a basis for flexible and dynamic negotiations. Given good will on both sides it will be possible soon to achieve a balanced result. It is our belief that we have not heard yet the last word from the Soviet Union.

We discussed in detail the CSCE follow-up meeting in Madrid. We continue to strive for an early substantial result, which would include an agreement on a conference on disarmament in Europe and make progress in the area of human rights. We also discussed the Vienna negotiations about mutual and balanced force reductions.

We had an extensive discussion about the whole field of East-West relations. We are agreed that personal contacts with the leaders of the Soviet Union continue to be important. We want to carry on our common efforts to arrive at constructive relations between East and West through dialogue and cooperation, wherever the Soviet Union makes this possible. We agreed on the need for continued efforts toward a common approach on East-West economic relations.

Another important subject we discussed was the preparation of the economic summit meeting to be held in Williamsburg at the end of May. In this context we exchanged views about the economic developments in our two countries and about measures to promote economic recovery. The summit meeting will provide us with an opportunity to intensify the emerging recovery of the international economy through close coordination. In this way we will be able, immediately prior to the continuation of the North-South dialogue at the UNCTAD Conference in Belgrade, to make a contribution towards solving the economic and social problems of the developing countries. Thus we want to promote their independence and genuine nonalignment.

I came to Washington also in my capacity as President-in-Office of the European Community. The President and I are agreed that the European Community and the United States together bear a great share of responsibility for the international economy. We are aware that the future development of relations between the United States and the European Community must and will live up to this responsibility.

I am leaving Washington firmly convinced that the quality of our relations will also in future determine our policy of safeguarding peace and, in particular, our common efforts to achieve progress in the Geneva negotiations.

41

Remarks by President Reagan in an Exchange of Toasts With President Carstens at a White House State Dinner, October 4, 1983

President Carstens and President Reagan on Carstens' arrival at the White House October 4, 1983, at the start of his state visit.

Federal President Karl Carstens visited the United States October 3 – 14, 1983, on the occasion of the tricentennial of German immigration to America. Stops on the tour included Washington, D.C.; Philadelphia; St. Louis; El Paso; Dallas; the Grand Canyon; Seattle; Madison, Wisconsin; New York and the United Nations; and New Haven. The official start of the visit was a state dinner at the White House, where President Reagan proposed the following toast:

Mr. President and Mrs. Carstens, Mr. Minister and Mrs. Genscher, honored guests. I said this morning and I would like to say it again how happy and proud that Nancy and I are to welcome you to the United States. Your own ties with our country, including a Master of Laws Degree from Yale University, are longstanding and deep.

Your life is a monument to the shared values and interests that have long provided our two peoples with a bounty of goodwill. And today, all Americans celebrate our ties and are grateful for our solid friendship with the German people.

Three hundred years ago, a small group of hardy pioneers set out from Krefeld in the Rhineland to sail into the unknown. In America they found the religious freedom they sought, but hard work was the price they paid for their newfound freedom. And those 13 German families brought with them courage and industry to build new lives. Their talents and those of their descendents helped create the great city of Philadelphia and the great state of Pennsylvania, both of which share our honor in welcoming you.

This year, we commemorate the remarkable odyssey of the Krefelders and of the millions of others who followed. The virtues of courage, industry and belief in freedom which they brought helped build our country, contributing to what is best about the United States. The contributions of German-Americans have been invaluable to the development of our great country.

The people of the Federal Republic of Germany have proven that they still possess those traits that helped build America. From the rubble of the Second World War the industrious German people constructed a strong, healthy and free democracy. We stand firmly together in the search for peace and freedom.

Anniversary celebrations tend to look back, but we should not limit our commemoration to reminiscences of the past. A strength of both of our peoples is that we also look to the future. The true meaning of this anniversary week is an enduring partnership that will lead to a more secure peace in the decades ahead.

Many colorful events have been organized throughout the United States to celebrate our ties. I congratulate the sponsors of these undertakings and of the numerous initiatives which have sprung up during this tricentennial year. The tricentennial reinvigorates the cultural, historical and political ties between our two peoples. It symbolizes something real, tangible and enduring—German-American friendship.

Mr. President, we're grateful for your visit. We thank you for all that you've personally done in your distinguished career to support close ties between our two nations. And I want to tell you, knowing your background here in America, when I was a boy I read about Frank Merriwell at Yale. I didn't read Brown of Harvard. (Laughter.) (Applause.)

We raise our glasses to you, Mr. President. To President Carstens and to the friendship that your visit represents.

42

Speech by President Carstens in Response to President Reagan's Remarks, October 4, 1983

In his response to President Reagan's toast, President Carstens emphasized the cordial bonds between the two countries:

Mr. President, Mrs. Reagan, ladies and gentlemen:

It gives me great pleasure, Mr. President, to be your guest here in the White House. I thank you most cordially, also in the name of my wife, of the Vice-Chancellor and Federal Foreign Minister and Mrs. Genscher, and of the other German guests, for the warm and generous hospitality which you are again extending to us.

I am deeply moved that it has been granted to me, as representative of the German people, to visit the United States and to strengthen the bonds of friendship with your great country. I look forward with eager expectation to the days in Philadelphia, St. Louis, Dallas, Seattle, Madison, New York and New Haven. Let us, Germans and Americans, bear in mind our common history; and let us take strength from our common ideals and our common goals.

On this visit, personal memories shall be accompanying me. I have been to the United States on numerous occasions in an official capacity. However, my thoughts go back above all to the time immediately after the Second World War when I obtained a scholarship from Yale University in 1948. The year which I spent there added a new dimension to my life. The goodwill and the cordiality which I encountered are firmly engraved in my memory. At Yale I studied American constitutional law, and I later qualified as a University Professor with a study on this subject. This aroused my interest in public affairs and in politics. I felt more and more called upon to work for the common good.

It also became clear to me at Yale as to what constitutes the real strength of the American nation, namely the conviction of its citizens that there are basic values which precede every governmental system. Among these values rank the dignity of man, justice and freedom; and also something which you, Mr. President, have repeatedly stressed, namely trust in God.

This has been true from the beginning. And the tricentennial of the first German immigration into North America marks an appropriate moment for recalling it.

"Proclaim freedom throughout the land for all its citizens." These words from the Book of Leviticus are inscribed on the Liberty

Bell in Philadelphia. In the first place, they referred to religious freedom; but they also referred to the other human rights, the "unalienable rights"—"life, liberty and the pursuit of happiness," as the Declaration of Independence expresses them.

In these ideals and the earnest endeavours to realize them lay the great attraction of the United States from the very beginning. Millions of Germans felt this attraction and went to America. They included many of our nation's best sons and daughters: freedom-loving, industrious and adventurous men and women who found a new home here. They became pioneers in building up your country, and they tied the cordial bonds of attachment between Germany and America which have proved their constancy despite severe setbacks. Germans played a role in the advance of American civilization, in the natural sciences, the social sciences, the fine arts and music—a civilization which has entered upon an unparalleled victorious march through the world in our epoch and which has profoundly influenced the lifestyle of almost all countries including, not least, that of Germany.

But the United States did not only lay a new foundation for social life within its own boundaries, but also in its relations towards other countries: "Observe good faith and justice towards all nations," declared George Washington in his farewell address; "cultivate peace and harmony with all ... to give to mankind the magnanimous and too novel example of a people always guided by an exalted justice and benevolence."

Clearly, it is difficult always to comply with such a high claim. However, benevolence and magnanimity remained guiding principles for American policy. We Germans also experienced this: the charitable assistance of the Americans after two world wars and the granting of economic aid in the shape of the Marshall Plan furnish examples of this, as does the Air Lift to Berlin, a city which owes so much to America and which you visited in June of last year, Mr. President.

Safeguarding freedom in Europe—that is the purpose of the North Atlantic Alliance in which our two countries are partners. This Alliance is a defence community, and there remains no need for me to stress that it only serves to defend. It is an Alliance among free peoples who have joined together because they share the same values, including freedom, which they wish to preserve.

This Alliance has granted us security and peace for over three decades. During this time, about nine million American citizens served as soldiers in Germany. Together with young German conscripts and troops from other member countries of the Alliance, they ensured that we can live in the manner desired by the overwhelming majority of our citizens, namely in a free democracy governed by the rule of law.

Germany is a divided country, yet we Germans adhere to the unity of our people. The policy pursued by the Federal Republic of Germany is directed towards a state of peace in Europe in which the German people will regain their unity through free self-determination. We thank America for always supporting this goal of ours.

For twenty years, the United States and the Federal Republic of Germany have been members of NATO.

If the Alliance endeavours to obtain a military equilibrium at as low a level as possible, this will guarantee not only freedom but also peace. Both of these—freedom and peace—would be endangered if the other side were to acquire military superiority. The fate of Afghanistan provides a sad example. We must never tire of pointing out these implications, time and time again, to those among our citizens who champion the cause of unilateral disarmament and whose motives I respect.

We Germans shall stand by your side as your allies and partners also in future.

And with this thought in mind, may I now raise my glass to drink to your health and success, Mr. President; to your health, Mrs. Reagan; to a happy future for the United States of America, the leading power among the free nations; and to another three centuries of German-American friendship!

43

Address by President Carstens to a Joint Session of Congress, October 5, 1983

President Carstens addressing a joint session of Congress, Washington, October 5, 1983. Seated behind President Carstens are Vice President Bush (left) and House Speaker O'Neill (right).

In an address to both Houses of Congress, President Carstens characterized German-American relations as based on partnership in the Atlantic Alliance, shared fundamental values, and a common heritage.

Mr. Speaker, Mr. Vice President, members of the
Congress of the United States:

Please accept my thanks, Mr. President, for the friendly words you have just addressed to me. I am grateful to you and to all the members of Congress that you have gathered for this meeting. I appreciate the honour of speaking to you and, through you, to the American people.

In this House the American citizen finds himself represented. Congress, together with the other great democratic institutions of this country, is at the same time guarantor of its freedom and a source of strength for its further dynamic development. In Senate

Joint Resolution 260, Congress has declared the year 1983 the "Tricentennial Anniversary Year of German Settlement in America."

This anniversary is, indeed, an event which stands out in the history of German-American relations, as it underlines the historical dimension of the bonds linking our two nations.

Let us seize this opportunity to remind ourselves of our common convictions and responsibilities. German immigration into your country began with the 13 families from Krefeld who set foot on American soil on October 6, 1683, in Philadelphia. They were followed in the course of the past three centuries by more than seven million Germans who left their homeland in search of freedom, protection from persecution and for a better life in the "new world."

The German immigrants have made their contribution to the development of the United States of America—as farmers and businessmen, as scientists and artists, as soldiers, teachers and politicians. America, which offered them a new home, became their fatherland. Their lives mirrored the words of Carl Schurz, who, an immigrant from the Rhineland, became a United States Senator and Secretary of the Interior, that "they could render no greater honour to their former fatherland than by becoming conscientious and faithful citizens of their new country."

Members of other nations have contributed as much to the development of the United States, and we realize that America increasingly has given us Germans a great deal in return. The shipments of food and clothing after World War II, the Marshall Plan, the Air Lift that saved Berlin, and the protective shield that America held over our young democracy will never be forgotten.

Twice in this century, relations between our two countries have been subjected to grave strains, but these strains were overcome, and a close friendship was born. It is a friendship founded on the kinship of our peoples. It is based on our common membership in the North Atlantic Alliance.

But, above all, it draws its stability from the common values on which the political and social order in our two countries is built: freedom, justice and democracy.

For us Germans there can only be partnership with the United States in the Alliance of free nations or dependence on the Soviet Union. We have made our choice.

Our understanding of democracy is based on the belief in the dignity and the rights of man. We trust in the power of the law to govern the life of men in a community.

And, finally, we are convinced that it is the duty of government to preserve internal and external peace, while guaranteeing the highest possible degree of responsibly exercised personal freedom.

Ladies and gentlemen, one glance beyond the open borders of Western civilization is sufficient to show us the power of attraction of our free democracies. The freedoms we enjoy remain an unfulfilled wish for many other peoples. The vision of these freedoms has, in the past centuries and up into our times, induced people from all parts of the world to take upon themselves the hardships of a long journey and the difficulties of a new beginning here in America.

For these same reasons, Germans from the other part of Germany are willing to risk their lives in order to overcome an unnatural and inhuman border and to escape to freedom.

We truly need not fear a contest of ideologies; we stand for principles which ensure freedom and lasting peace, among them: self-determination of men and nations.

By virtue of this right of self-determination ten countries in Europe have formed a community. After centuries of war and bitterness, a network of close relations has emerged among them. The German-French friendship assumes a singular position in this process.

From the beginning, America has supported European unification, recognizing that a strong, united Western Europe would be a valuable partner for America.

The United States bears world responsibility. You did not seek this responsibility, but as the strongest among the free nations you accepted it in the interest of our common future.

By virtue of their right of self-determination and in response to external danger, 14 European nations, together with the United States and Canada, united to form the Atlantic Alliance. It is a purely defensive alliance; it is incapable of waging a war of aggression. It is the most efficient alliance of modern times.

It is to this alliance that its members owe more than 30 years of peace and freedom. America's commitment to Europe was confirmed by President Reagan only last year when he spoke to the German Bundestag and said, "Europe's shores are our shores. Europe's borders are our borders."

We know that America, given its engagement in Europe, rightly expects partnership and a reasonable distribution of burdens. The Federal Republic of Germany has proven in the past that it is prepared to meet these expectations and will continue to contribute its fair share to the common defence. It will live up to its commitments. You can rely on us, as we rely on you.

We have 500,000 soldiers under arms, well-equipped, well-trained and willing, if necessary, to defend our country together with our allies.

Let me say a few words about the American soldiers in Germany. Within an area which in size corresponds approximately to the state of Oregon, there are, in addition to half a million German soldiers, 350,000 soldiers from six NATO countries; 250,000 of these are Americans. It is unavoidable that such a concentration also creates difficulties for the soldiers and for the population. Life in an environment which is foreign to them is not always easy for American servicemen and their families.

Therefore, I would like to emphasize that the American soldiers and their dependents are welcome in our country as our friends and as allies. We know that we owe to their presence our security, our freedom and peace, and in saying this, I speak for the great majority of our people.

To safeguard peace today is of greater importance than ever before. To reach that goal we must keep a balance of power. We want a balance at the lowest possible level of armaments.

This policy, however, has come under criticism in our countries. In view of the terrifying effects of nuclear weapons, many of our citizens demand their abolition, and some demand, if need be, their unilateral abolition. Although I can understand such feelings, I do not share the conclusions. My experience has taught me that good intentions alone are not enough to preserve peace. We are dealing with a highly armed superpower which is making great efforts in order to increase its influence in many parts of the world.

The fate of Afghanistan shows us what may happen to a country which is not able to defend itself. Therefore, the Alliance, in striving for a balance of military power, secures not only freedom, but also peace. We must not tire of pointing out this connection to those among our countrymen who—sometimes very emotionally—advocate unilateral disarmament and whose motives I respect.

I am convinced that the Alliance can protect life, liberty and peace if we maintain and, where necessary, restore our ability to defend ourselves, while being ready to enter into agreements on arms control and disarmament at the lowest possible level.

When I speak of defence, I do not mean confrontation. On the contrary, we in the Federal Republic of Germany have tried to build bridges between east and west in order to reduce tension and, if possible, to improve conditions for the peoples in Eastern Europe. We did this in full agreement with our Western Allies, and we shall continue our efforts along this line.

We, the United States of America and the Federal Republic of Germany, are also partners at the Conference for Security and Cooperation in Europe; here we are working for the realization of human rights throughout Europe.

In making this point I am conscious of speaking to you as a representative of a divided nation which is painfully aware of the fact that freedom, rule of law and democracy are denied to the other part of Germany. We trust that the unnatural division of our country, which at the same time divides Europe, will not last. The wall cannot and will not be history's final verdict. We are grateful that the United States endorses the political aim of the Federal Republic of Germany to work for a state of peace in Europe in which the German nation will regain its unity through free self-determination.

Tensions result not only from East-West relations. We are also concerned about the development of the world economy. At the meeting of the Heads of State and Government from seven industrial nations which took place in Williamsburg at the invitation of the President of the United States last May it was agreed that it is a matter of common endeavour and responsibility to work for recovery in order to ensure, on the basis of sustained and lasting economic rehabilitation, new jobs and a better life for the people of our own countries and of the world.

We will overcome our present difficulties only by working together. This also means that we must show consideration in dealing with one another and take no unilateral measures which could harm the other partners.

Ladies and gentlemen, German-American friendship and partnership have now lasted over a generation, and they will remain the foundation of our policy in the future. But as relations between individuals demand constant attention, good relations between nations must not be taken for granted. We must enable our young people—on both sides of the Atlantic—to become better acquainted with the other country and their peers. They ought to have the chance to understand that young people, here as well as there, share values and interests, anxieties and hopes; that their lives rest on the same foundation. We, therefore, vigorously support President Reagan's initiative to intensify the youth exchange between our two countries. In the coming days, I myself will be speaking at universities in St. Louis, Seattle, Madison and at Yale. I especially welcome the creation of an exchange-sponsorship programme marking the tricentennial celebrations. It is a programme sponsored by the Congress of the United States and the German Bundestag, designed to pave the way for more personal encounters between young Americans and Germans. I am pleased that Mrs. Renger, Vice-President of the German Bundestag, will present a document to this effect following this meeting.

Ladies and gentlemen, let me conclude: American-German friendship is founded:

- on the German contribution to the building of the American nation,
- on the unforgotten help which America gave us after World War II,
- on America's commitment to Berlin's freedom,
- on our partnership in the Atlantic Alliance, which is guaranteeing freedom and peace in our part of the world,
- on our common commitment to a sound world economy,
- and above all: on fundamental values which we share: democracy, individual liberty and the rule of law.

Let us stand together in this spirit. It is the best contribution we can make to ensuring future generations a life in freedom and peace.

44

Speech by President Carstens at the
Tricentennial Banquet in Philadelphia,
October 6, 1983

The ceremonial highlight of President Carstens' visit was a banquet in Philadelphia commemorating the landing of the first German immigrants 300 years earlier. In his address, the Federal President spoke of the common German-American heritage:

Mr. Vice-President, Mrs. Bush, Mr. Governor, honorable members
of the Senate, honorable members of the House of
Representatives, Mr. Beichl, deutsche Landsleute,
ladies and gentlemen:

It is a pleasure for me to be here and to commemorate with you the day on which, 300 years ago, thirteen families from Krefeld landed on the banks of the Delaware after a 75-day ocean voyage.

I am happy, Mr. Vice-President, that you are attending this festive banquet. You were in Krefeld last summer, from where those thirteen families had set out. Nothing could better demonstrate the significance your country attributes to the part German immigrants played in building up America than your presence last summer in Krefeld and here tonight.

My thanks also go to those who have planned and organized this splendid banquet—vor allem Ihnen, Herr Professor Beichl, und den Damen und Herren der German Society of Pennsylvania, danke ich. Nicht nur, daß Sie diesen festlichen Abend mit grenzenloser Hingabe und harter Arbeit vorbereitet haben—,Sie haben auch eine Reihe von zusätzlichen Feiern in ganz Pennsylvanien veranstaltet.

I must ask for your understanding that I have spoken a few sentences in German. I wanted to thank Professor Beichl and the members of the German Society in the language of their forefathers for the preparation of this evening as well as for what they have contributed to German-American friendship.

I visited Germantown this afternoon, and in the museum there I got an impression of the beginnings of German settlement. Religious motives had induced the German emigrants to leave their old home and to found a new one here. Upon their arrival they were met by goodwill, tolerance and trust. Together with the many others who came after them, they have not disappointed those who welcomed them with open arms.

One hundred years ago, in 1883, when the bicentennial anniversary of German immigration was commemorated, there were countless festivals and celebrations in this country. The German immigrants' contribution to the growth and flourishing of the United States was praised in many speeches.

World War I brought a deep rupture in German-American relations. It also put many Americans of German ancestry to a difficult test. The National Socialist regime, in its contempt of human life, and the Second World War once again seriously burdened relations. But it was possible to overcome both these setbacks.

Beginning immediately after the war's end, Americans sent more than 16 million CARE parcels to Germany. The Marshall Plan, that magnificent and unparalleled project, helped our economy back onto its feet. By means of the Air Lift, a further unprecedented undertaking, Berlin's freedom was rescued. And today America is our ally in the North Atlantic Alliance, is the indispensable shield for freedom and peace.

What were the reasons for this willingness to help, which stands in such contrast to previous historical experience? One was the natural generosity characteristic of the American people.

Another reason can be found in the impressions Americans gained in Germany after 1945. The soldiers who where stationed there met the Germans with understanding and sympathy, often even compassion, and finally they became friends.

Another reason was the good reputation German-Americans had earned in their new fatherland. They remained fond of their old home country, yet had become Americans through and through. They had proven themselves as farmers and businessmen, as teachers and scientists, soldiers and politicians, and they had helped to move the United States to a leading position among nations.

We are pleased about what President Reagan on various occasions and what you, Mr. Vice-President, said regarding the contribution of the German immigrants, as well as about the recognition expressed in Senate Joint Resolution No. 260. We are especially grateful to you, Senator Heinz, for having given the initial impulse for this resolution.

In your letter to me, you and Senator Specter have mentioned the bonds uniting our two nations: democratic ideals, a dense network of economic and cultural relations, and the common commitment we share as allies to defend the freedom and the values today enjoyed by both our peoples. I can only agree with you, and I hope that, on both sides of the Atlantic, we—and the younger generations as well—will always remain conscious of this community of destiny.

The Liberty Bell in Berlin, a replica of the Liberty Bell in your city, carries the inscription: "That this world under God shall have a new birth of freedom." In 1776, when the Liberty Bell rang out the independence of the United States, no one could say with certainty when freedom would be won—just as today no one can say with certainty when and how freedom and human dignity will overcome the powers of oppression from which many people suffer.

We are convinced that the idea of freedom is stronger than those ideologies which, in the semblance of spreading human happiness, lead to oppression.

We want to hold fast to our convictions and do our part so that ever more people may live in peace and freedom.

In this age-old struggle, freedom will prevail, not by force but through its spiritual strength. We stand for liberty and self-determination, for justice and the rule of law, for government by the people through their freely elected representatives. We stand for the cause of peace—peace within our countries and outside.

There is no better system.

It attracts people from all over the world, and those states which deny basic human rights to their citizens have to use force and coercion in order to prevent them from leaving their own country.

The appeal of freedom is as strong today as it was 300 years ago.

With these thoughts in mind, I raise my glass to the health of President Reagan, to your health, Mr. Vice-President, to the health of all those present, to German-American friendship!

45

Speech by President Carstens at Carnegie Hall, New York, October 13, 1983

On October 13, 1983, President Carstens addressed an audience gathered at Carnegie Hall in New York for a concert of Beethoven music by the Bamberg Symphony Orchestra. Among the other guests of honor were John J. McCloy, former American high commissioner in Germany, and Undersecretary of State Lawrence Eagleburger.

Mr. McCloy, Mr. Undersecretary of State, Mr. Kaletsch,
ladies and gentlemen:

I am grateful to you, Mr. McCloy, and to you, Mr. Undersecretary of State, for your kind words; and I am also grateful to the ladies and gentlemen of the German Forum for organizing this outstanding event in the famous Carnegie Hall.

My visit, which has taken me across the whole American continent, to seven states and now to New York, is drawing to a close.

It was a magnificent visit. I had long talks with President Reagan, he gave us a splendid dinner in the White House. I conferred with the Secretary of State. I addressed both Houses of Congress and my speech was very warmly received.

I talked, together with Vice-President Bush, to 2,000 people in Philadelphia, where both of us evoked the German contribution to the building of the American nation as well as our long-standing friendship. And I conferred in St. Louis, El Paso, Dallas, Seattle, Madison, Wisconsin, and New York with political leaders, businessmen, scientists, artists, soldiers and students. All this made a deep impression on me.

But what impressed me even more was the spirit I encountered: the vitality, the dynamism and the optimism of the American people as well as its unbroken democratic tradition, which now dates back more than 200 years. Believe me, this is unique in the world. It is the real source of your strength, on which I congratulate you. In saying this, I am aware of grave social problems which your country faces and of which I have been informed.

The occasion of my state visit is the 300th anniversary of German immigration into the United States.

For 230 years thereafter, relations between Germany and America were unclouded. Many Germans—in fact over seven million of them—found an opportunity here of living in accordance with their religious and political convictions; of building a better life for themselves; and of making a fresh start. In return, they brought along their skills, their energy, their good will. President Reagan said quite recently: "Without Germany, we would not be what we are." I do not say this in order to boast: we know that other nations have contributed just as much or even more to the growth of America. But we are pleased that our compatriots' contribution is recognized.

The First World War brought a severe setback in our relations, and many Americans of German extraction went through a difficult time even though they were loyal citizens of their new homeland. The National Socialist regime and the Second World War again generated grave tensions. It was during this period that the United States gave shelter to thousands of Germans who had to leave Germany because they were persecuted. We shall never forget this, we shall always be grateful to your country for it. But we are grateful also to the immigrants, who after the collapse of the Nazi dictatorship took a leading part in helping Germany and in reconciling our two peoples.

A new phase of history began. The Americans showed to their defeated adversaries the benevolence and magnanimity which George Washington had recommended to his people. There are few parallels in history to the CARE parcels, the Marshall Plan, the Air Lift which rescued Berlin—and to America's support in rebuilding German democracy after the war.

In this context I want to mention two men: General Lucius D. Clay, who proposed the Air Lift to Berlin and carried full responsibility for its operation, and John J. McCloy, who as the American High Commissioner helped us when we laid the new democratic foundations for the Federal Republic of Germany. Both names will always be remembered in our country with profound gratitude. They will go down into the history both of the United States and of Germany as great statesmen who showed courage and wisdom in an hour of trial. Under Chancellor Konrad Adenauer, with whom they worked closely together, the Federal Republic of Germany took the historic decision to tie its destiny to the free countries of the West. The policy of European integration and of German-French reconciliation began which produced so many remarkable results during the following decades.

For almost 30 years the Federal Republic has been a member of the North Atlantic Alliance and our two countries have become allies and friends. Occasionally our relations have been marked by difficulties, inadequate consultation and a lack of mutual consideration. However, the difficulties were overcome, and that will also be the case in future. We must speak frankly to each other, as friend to friend: we must remain conscious that what links us together is incomparably more important and stronger than what divides us, namely—to quote President Reagan—"The values we hold, the beliefs we cherish, the ideals to which we are dedicated," i.e., democracy and justice, the freedom of Man, his dignity and his inalienable rights. These rights are still denied to the other part of our people. Our nation is still divided. But we are convinced that the unnatural frontier will not be history's last verdict, and we shall continue to work for a state of peace in Europe in which the whole German nation regains its freedom and self-determination. We are grateful to the United States for having always supported this policy.

Recently criticism of the security policy of the Atlantic Alliance has been voiced in both our countries. Some of our fellow citizens demand complete abolition of all nuclear weapons and, if an agreement cannot be reached, even their unilateral abolition by our side. I respect the motives of those who argue in good faith, but I firmly believe that peace and freedom would be in danger if the other side gained military superiority. Many experiences in history, of which Afghanistan is the latest, should warn us against having illusions.

To those who advocate unilateral disarmament we should repeat without tiring that the Atlantic Alliance is a purely defensive alliance. We must also point to the great efforts we are making to reach disarmament agreements with the Soviet Union. We want a military equilibrium on the lowest possible level. But we must maintain an equilibrium of military forces, otherwise we would lose the capability to defend ourselves. I have personally no doubt that this is a sound and realistic policy. But I would like on this occasion to say a few words on behalf of those Germans who hold a different view.

Our country, the Federal Republic of Germany, is approximately of the same size as the state of Oregon. It has 60 million inhabitants; Oregon has about 2 million. 850,000 soldiers are stationed in our country. 500,000 Germans, 250,000 Americans and also British, French, Canadian, Dutch and Belgian troops. Several thousand nuclear warheads are already deployed on our soil. I think if people under such circumstances are afraid of the deployment of still more missiles, that is an understandable, though in my view irrational, reaction.

In my opinion, our most important task lies in passing on the experience gathered by my generation to the young generation of today. The values to which I have been referring will only retain their strength if they are adopted and renewed by our young people.

It is good to see German and American soldiers standing side by side, and I want to take this opportunity to thank in the name of the vast majority of our people the American soldiers for the great service they render the cause of freedom and of peace. We regard them as our allies, partners and friends.

I am pleased that the German Bundestag and the American Congress adopted a new exchange programme a few days ago, and I would ask you to do your utmost to ensure that many young Americans get to know Europe. When I return to Germany, I shall again make every effort to induce young Germans to go to America for a few months or a year.

If our two peoples and the free nations continue to stand together, then there will be no need to indulge in pessimism.

We stand for the better cause; in the long run it will prevail over the forces of oppression. Then we shall be able to give more people on earth the chance of leading a fuller life. Then we shall be able to safeguard peace and to help ensure, in the words inscribed on the Berlin Liberty Bell, that "This world under God shall have a new birth of freedom."

This is the sentiment which Beethoven, who was born in Bonn, will now convey to us. May his Seventh Symphony, first preformed 170 years ago, imbue us with a sense of unity, of courage and further inspiration.

Sources

1. Germany (Federal Republic, 1949–   ), *Journey to America; Collected Speeches, Statements, Press, Radio and TV Interviews by Dr. Konrad Adenauer, Chancellor, Federal Republic of Germany, During His Visit to the United States and Canada, April 6–18, 1953* (Washington, D.C.: Press Office, German Diplomatic Mission, n.d.), pp. 15–16.

2. Ibid., pp. 75–81.

3. Germany (Federal Republic, 1949–   ), Presse- und Informationsamt, *Bulletin des Presse- und Informationsamtes der Bundesregierung,* Nr. 207, Nov. 8, 1954, pp. 1856–1857. Translation by German Information Center, New York.

4. The White House and The German Embassy, Joint Press Release, Washington, D.C., June 14, 1955.

5. German Embassy, Press Release, Washington, D.C., June 11, 1956.

6. U.S., Congress, Senate, Visit to the Senate by His Excellency Konrad Adenauer, Chancellor of the Federal Republic of Germany, 85th Congress, 1st sess., May 27, 1957, *Congressional Record* 103: 7837–7838.

7. Press Office of the German Embassy, Press Release, Washington, D.C., May 28, 1957.

8. The White House and the German Federal Press Office, Joint Press Release, May 28, 1957.

9. U.S., President, *Public Papers of the Presidents of the United States* (Washington, D.C.: Office of the *Federal Register,* National Archives and Records Service, 1953–   ), Dwight D. Eisenhower, 1958, § 126, p. 456.

10. U.S., Congress, House, Address by His Excellency Theodor Heuss, President of the Federal Republic of Germany, 85th Congress, 2nd sess., June 5, 1958, *Congressional Record* 104: 10311–10313.

11. U.S., President, Public Papers of the Presidents of the United States (Washington, D.C.: Office of the *Federal Register,* National Archives and Records Service, 1953–   ), Dwight D. Eisenhower, 1959, § 192, pp. 616–617.

12. *New York Times,* November 23, 1961, p. 4.

13. U.S., President, *Public Papers of the Presidents of the United States* (Washington, D.C.: Office of the *Federal Register,* National Archives and Records Service, 1953–   ), John F. Kennedy, 1963, § 253, pp. 497–498.

14. U.S., President, *Public Papers of the Presidents of the United States* (Washington, D.C.: Office of the *Federal Register,* National Archives and Records Service, 1953–   ), John F. Kennedy, 1963, § 261, pp. 511–512.

15. Ibid., § 262, pp. 512–513.

16. O. M. Artus, *President John F. Kennedy in Germany: A Documentation* (Heiligenhaus, Richard Bärenfeld-Verlag, 1965), pp. 158–168.

17. Germany (Federal Republic, 1949–   ) 7 Press and Information Office of the German Federal Government, *The Bulletin,* vol. 11, no. 24 (July 1963), pp. 1–2.

18. Germany (Federal Republic, 1949–   ), German Embassy, Washington, D.C., *News From the German Embassy,* vol. 8, no. 10 (June 1964).

19. *Weekly Compilation of Presidential Documents* 3 (October 3, 1966): 1359–1360.

20. *Weekly Compilation of Presidential Documents* 3 (October 3, 1966): 1367–1371.

21. *Weekly Compilation of Presidential Documents* 3 (August 21, 1967): 1154–1157.

22. *Weekly Compilation of Presidential Documents* 5 (March 3, 1969): 323.

23. *Weekly Compilation of Presidential Documents* 6 (April 13, 1970): 507–508.

24. *Weekly Compilation of Presidential Documents* 6 (April 13, 1970): 509–510.

25. Germany (Federal Republic, 1949–   ), German Information Center, New York, *The Marshall Plan and the Future of U.S.-European Relations* (New York, German Information Center, 1972), pp. 13–24.

26. *Weekly Compilation of Presidential Documents* 10 (December 9, 1974): 1534–1536.

27. *Weekly Compilation of Presidential Documents* 11 (June 16, 1975): 632–634.

28. U.S., Congress, House, Joint Meeting of the Two Houses of Congress to Receive the President of the Federal Republic of Germany, Walter Scheel, 94th Congress, 1st sess., June 17, 1975, *Congressional Record* 121: 19149–19151.

29. *Weekly Compilation of Presidential Documents* 11 (August 4, 1975): 793–794.

30. Germany (Federal Republic, 1949–), Press and Information Office, *The Bulletin*, Archive Supplement, vol. 3, no. 7 (Bonn, 1976), pp. 5–6.

31. U.S., President, *Public Papers of the Presidents of the United States* (Washington, D.C.: Office of the *Federal Register*, National Archives and Records Service, 1953–), Jimmy Carter, 1977, Book 2, pp. 1246–1248.

32. U.S., President, *Public Papers of the Presidents of the United States* (Washington, D.C.: Office of the *Federal Register*, National Archives and Records Service, 1953–), Jimmy Carter, 1978, Book 2, pp. 1286–1289.

33. *Weekly Compilation of Presidential Documents* 17 (May 25, 1981): 546–548.

34. Ibid., pp. 552–554.

35. U.S., Department of State, Bureau of Public Affairs, *Alliance Security and Arms Control*, By Ronald Reagan, Current Policy No. 400 (Washington, D.C.), United States Department of State, Bureau of Public Affairs, Washington, D.C., June 1982).

36. The White House, Office of the Press Secretary, Press Release, West Berlin, June 11, 1982.

37. The White House, Office of the Press Secretary, Press Release, Washington, D.C., November 15, 1982.

38. Germany (Federal Republic, 1949–), German Information Center, "Joint Statement of President Reagan and West German Chancellor Kohl in Washington on November 16, 1982," *Statements and Speeches*, vol. 5, no. 24 (New York, German Information Center, November 19, 1982).

39. German Information Center, Press Release, New York, November 16, 1982.

40. The White House, Press Release, Washington, D.C., April 15, 1983.

41. The White House, Office of the Press Secretary, Press Release, Washington, D.C., October 4, 1983.

42. Germany (Federal Republic, 1949–), Presse- und Informationsamt der Bundesregierung, *Bulletin*, Nr. 117, Nov. 4, 1983, pp. 1057–1058.

43. Ibid., pp. 1059–1061.

44. Ibid., pp. 1065–1066.

45. Ibid., pp. 1072–1074.

Note: The statements and speeches appearing in this book have been reproduced as they appear in the sources cited above except for minor editing by the German Information Center to correct obvious typographical errors or variances from standard usage.